THE REAL AVIA ENTHUSIAST

Peter R March

ROYAL AIR FORCE BENEVOLENT FUND ENTERPRISES

THE REAL AVIATION ENTHUSIAST II

Published by The Royal Air Force
Benevolent Fund Enterprises,
Building 15, RAF Fairford,
Glos GL7 4DL, England

Publishing Director: Paul A. Bowen
Compiled & Edited: Peter R. March
Contributors: Lindsay Peacock, Hugh Lohan, Gordon Bartley & anon
Cartoons: Hugh Lohan, Tim Newman
Photographs: Peter R. March (PRM) and as credited
Editorial Assistant: Brian Strickland
Typesetting and Design: Karin Willis
Cover artwork: Hugh Lohan
Cover design: Graham Finch

The words printed in the Real Aviation Enthusiast II are those of the various authors and contributors alone and bear little relationship to the REAL truth. No reflection of the policies of The Royal Air Force Benevolent Fund Enterprises, is either implied or intended.

ISBN 0 9516581 9 0 2nd revised and enlarged edition
(ISBN 0 9511665 0 6 1st edition 1987)

© The Royal Air Force Benevolent Fund Enterprises 1995

Printed in Hong Kong

Foreword

by Air Chief Marshal Sir Roger Palin KCB OBE MA FRAeS FIPD - Controller of
The Royal Air Force Benevolent Fund and Chairman, International Air Tattoo

When I first read this book in galley form it struck me all over again how humour cannot be beaten as an antidote to taking life too seriously. I suppose that we aviation enthusiasts can appear rather an eccentric lot, prepared to put up with any amount of discomfort in pursuit of our particular Holy Grail. This sort of dedication can sometimes lead to an overly earnest approach, but at heart we all know that we do it because it's fun. And that's what this second edition of The REAL Aviation Enthusiast, like the first, is all about.

The inspiration behind the first edition was Bryan Philpott, a man of great wit and perception who sadly died on 1 March 1989. REAL Aviation Enthusiast II is a testament to the best of his work, and has been compiled and edited by Peter March who has spent decades observing, and indeed taking part in, the cut and thrust of the aviation world. With new material from Lindsay Peacock and Hugh Lohan, the book never loses its light touch as it takes a wry look at the aviologist at work.

One thing that I am particularly proud of is that thousands of "REAL Aviation Enthusiasts" volunteer every year to help run International Air Tattoo, since 1976 the Fund's flagship event. As the new millennium approaches many veterans of war face their most vulnerable years, and the commitment of the IAT volunteer team takes on an even greater significance. The money they work so hard to raise for the Fund's work helps us to look after those in need.

Since forming in 1919 as the Royal Air Force Memorial Fund, under the unerring guidance of Lord Hugh Trenchard, we have brought comfort to over 820,000 members of the extended RAF family, men and women of all ranks who have served in war or peace, their families and their dependants.

We were all very touched recently to receive a letter from Rachel who is thirteen years old. Her father, a 41-year-old sergeant personnel administrator went down with pneumonia. Complications and consequent surgery left him an invalid - and he had to leave the RAF prematurely. Rachel says "I thought you would like it if I told you about the lovely house we are all living in thanks to your kindness......If it hadn't been for the Benevolent Fund I hate to think what would of happened to us. Thanks a million".

Rachel is really thanking all of you who support the Fund. In buying this book you have helped to make sure that we can go on answering the call of Royal Air Force men and women - serving or long retired - who turn to us in times of need or distress. I hope that you enjoy The REAL Aviation Enthusiast II as much as I did.

Roger Palin

Introduction

The Real Aviation Enthusiast I came from the pen of the late Bryan Philpott in 1987, who was at that time the Press Officer for the Royal Air Force Benevolent Fund's International Air Tattoo. He said in his Preface to that first edition: *'The idea for this book first came to me during the TVS Airshow South at Hurn Airport in 1984. Just outside the Press Centre was parked a Breguet Alizé; its wings were folded and it sat in that rather quaint manner that naval aircraft seem to adopt. Long after the flying had finished, a family group wandered along and stood taking in all the details of this specimen of French aviation. Mum, with the youngest cradled in her arms, was clearly anxious to get home, but dad, complete with his Kodak Instamatic, binoculars and picnic box, and a young lad on each hand, wanted his full money's worth. "What's that dad?" enquired one of the lads, pointing his ice lolly at the Alizé.*

"A Royal Navy Gannet", was the immediate answer. Meanwhile the other small son had wandered over to the enclosure. "Is it?" he asked me, clearly doubting dad but not wanting to question his authority. "Actually, it's an Alizé", I whispered.

Small boy immediately rushed over to dad shouting, "No it's not, THAT man..." pointing an accusing finger in my general direction, "says it's a Lizzie".

Dad looked horror-struck. "Take no notice of HIM lad. A Lizzie was a World War 2 plane with wings coming out of the top of the cockpit and a big radial engine...THAT's a Gannet!" Whereupon the whole family turned as one and moved off towards a nearby Jet Provost; my little friend turned towards me and poked his tongue out!

Such groups are what air shows are all about. They are the multitude who make it all worthwhile, they demand nothing more than a day out in the sun, a lot of interesting things to look at and occupy their time, a spot to sit and enjoy their flasks of tea and sandwiches, and a quiet wander round to see how their taxes are being spent. They make the world of air shows possible and a mecca for that small minority of experts, who without any doubt are very knowledgeable, but can also be very painful'.

Hugh Lohan, a fellow IATer produced his very personal cartoons and with photographs from the present compiler, Bryan Philpott put together an original and very popular best seller that he dedicated 'to all aviation enthusiasts wherever they might be!'.

The years have rolled by and the whole aviation world has changed very dramatically with the collapse of communism, upheavals in the Middle East and southern Europe. But despite all this the REAL aviation enthusiast is still out there hard at work. Airshows have also changed, there are now aircraft appearing at UK shows that back in 1987 we would not have thought possible. Just look at the MiGs, Mils, Sukhois and Yaks that are now part of the UK air display scene. Not just at Farnborough, but at Fairford, Biggin Hill, Waddington and Woodford.

Once again we can turn back to Bryan Philpott's Introduction to underline the raison d'être for this second edition. 'Most of us become so engrossed in our jobs, hobbies and pastimes, that too frequently we overlook the fact that there is always a humorous element close at hand. There is a danger of losing sight of this completely and taking ourselves far too seriously, and when this happens a lot of pleasure can go from our lives. Humour is, of course, a very personal thing; what appeals to one person may not appeal to another, but quite often there is a common ground and in the world of aviation this can take many forms'.

This second edition has been brought together from the best of the original material, some previously unpublished cartoons by Hugh Lohan, and much new text supplied by arch enthusiast Lindsay Peacock and the compiler. The photographs have come mainly from the March family vaults, together with Peter and Richard Cooper, Brian Strickland, Richard L. Ward, Lindsay Peacock and IAT files.

This book once again lifts the lid off some of the people, situations and aircraft that are all out there making up the aviation world of the mid-90s. No one individual nor any organisation should take personal offence at anything that is said, or implied, about them in this book. There is no malice intended in any way. Nobody is above some light-hearted banter or even ridicule – and no-one escapes it in the REAL AVIATION ENTHUSIAST II – not even the compiler (who originally came in for some attention in the first edition).

It is about time that aviation enthusiasts had a mirror held up to them again – and if they are able to recognise themselves in it we have been successful!

We are all indebted to Bryan Philpott for the original idea and hope that this new edition of his book reflects that REAL enthusiast's humour.

Special thanks must go to the following for their assistance with the supply of material for The REAL Aviation Enthusiast II: Gordon Bartley, Sue Bushell, Peter & Richard Cooper, Phil Coulson, Paul Jackson, Hugh Lohan, Andrew & Daniel March, Lindsay Peacock, David Stephens, Brian Strickland and Karin Willis.

Peter R. March, May 1995

Aeroplane

Well, we do have to begin with this word as that's what the book's all about. And Bryan began the first edition this way trying (and failing) to find a satisfactory definition. Like so many things in this book it poses more questions than it answers, but that is an inherent part of the REAL aviation enthusiast's philosophy, as you are about to find out.

What is an aeroplane? To a greater or lesser extent most dictionaries (except the one that you've got) define an 'aeroplane' as a 'heavier-than-air flying machine with fixed wings and mechanical propulsion systems that provide sufficient forward motion to allow the lift that is generated by the wings to exceed the force of gravity'. Well, that sounds all nice and technically straightforward. This immediately excludes all helicopters, gliders, manpowered flying machines and even the Harrier. Go tell that to Bill Bedford or the brothers at Kingston. To describe them all as having fixed wings is another contradiction. If you have sat in view of the wing, while flying to the Costas in an Airbus 300 on a hot summer's (sorry on *the* hot summer's) day, you will know that wings do actually move while in flight. They don't flap about to any great degree – other than on the Airbus A-330/340 or Boeing 747. The exception that proves the rule is of course the B-52. Next time the *Buffs* visit Fairford just compare the droop of the B-52's wings while on the ground, with its noticeably up-turned wings when in the air.

Now we have eliminated half of the definition we're left with 'heavier-than-air flying machine'. This sounds fair enough, until

'707 jumping the lights again at 250mph. That's another three points and £1500 for the tea fund.' PRM

you look more closely at some of the things that you see flying through the air these days – motor-bikes, cars, vans – particularly if you live in California. You certainly couldn't call some of the heavier than air 'flying' machines in use at certain massage parlours, aeroplanes.

Most REAL aviation enthusiasts have little time for such analytical clap-trap. They use the generic term 'aircraft' to describe the species (such as those boring Boeings, Bulldogs or Blue Circle F3s) and give the accolade 'aeroplane' to those real machines that they consider to be worth thinking about. Every enthusiast will have a top 20+ checklist of REAL aeroplanes. If

The REAL aviation enthusiast starts young.

OBVIOUSLY NOT EVERYONE IN WALES APPRECIATES AVIATION!

Low flying RAF aircraft are popular wherever they appear! BAe

you haven't actually got one sorted out, you had better do it now, or you won't qualify for the ultimate accolade when you get to the end of this book.

Where are you likely to encounter REAL aeroplanes? The answer is just about anywhere apart from airports (they're too expensive to land at), in the air over major cities (not allowed to fly there especially if it's only got one engine), over Tory Party conferences (they might be up to no good – the pilots that is), any heliport, on a really foggy day, any underground car park, any reputable zoo, banks and building societies (unless they have seized them from the devoted owners).

The great Arthur Daly syndrome has permeated into the British aviation culture. Thankfully wherever you travel, by whatever means, you can expect to come across aeroplanes. It might be in a farmer's field somewhere in Wales, down a glen in Scotland or behind the silage heap in East Anglia. Look over the hedge as you drive into Cirencester and you might see a Fairey Gannet, or a Hawker Hunter in the Home Counties. With so much more low flying around the British Isles now that the Germans have decided they don't want us in their airspace (or anyone else come to that), you can expect to have your happy holiday pleasantly interrupted by a low-flying REAL military aeroplane.

Aircraft

Having come to grief in trying to define an aeroplane, let's take an easier course of action and seek the advice of super-spotter and editor of *Jane's All the Worlds Aircraft*, Paul Jackson, for his learned definition. His theory of flying machines goes roughly like this: 'All aeroplanes or helicopters are aircraft, but not all aircraft are aeroplanes or helicopters. All aeroplanes are not helicopters but are aircraft, while all helicopters are aircraft but aren't aeroplanes. Aircraft that are not aeroplanes or helicopters are balloons, airships or autogiros. All aircraft are able to fly but not all flying objects are aircraft. Flying objects that are capable of controlled flight that are not aircraft include birds and bats – flying objects that are not capable of controlled flight include dead birds and cricket bats. The latter do not so much fly as plummet, but not all plummeting objects are dead birds and cricket bats, since both aircraft and birds are capable of this act. I am not at all sure where flying fish fit in to all this, but I have learned never to stand in the way of any plummeting object.' Thank you Mr Jackson – ask a silly question and you get......

'I think I've found out why this Lightning won't fly.' LINDSAY PEACOCK

Aerobatics

When REAL aeroplanes were first flown, their pilots had only one thing in mind – to take off, fly straight and level from A to B and back again, with the minimum of discomfort and maximum safety for themselves and those below them on the ground. This continued until early in the First World War when a German fighter ace on a patrol over the Western Front dropped his flying instruction manual between his legs. Reaching down to retrieve it he pushed the control column forward and went into a vertical dive, the book flew upwards with the negative g, so the desperate pilot (who needed it to tell him what to do if he saw a Royal Flying Corps machine heading his way – and how to land the plane back behind the German lines) violently pulled back on the stick to try to prevent the book from departing into space. Painfully, the control stick got caught in his trousers which he had loosened shortly before to produce the contents of a bottle that he intended should add to the discomfort of the British troops in the trenches.

These poor unfortunates were to witness the first, and without a shadow of doubt the most spectacular, aerobatic display to be given in a powered aircraft. One Tommy wrote in his diary 'this plane rolled around the sky, sometimes going straight up and then coming vertically down again. The pilot was enjoying himself, we could hear him shouting out numbers and singing – he threw books and a bottle of orange juice down to us (sadly it broke when it hit the ground). It went on for about ten minutes. Then his engine stopped and he drifted down to land a couple of fields away from us. The troops all clapped and cheered at his display. When they pulled him from his plane that had ended up on its nose in the boggy field, all he asked for was his book back. The other strange thing was that his trousers got left hooked over the pilot's control stick in the plane. We asked him his name, in case we should later find his book, and he said it was Baron von Loop de Loupe'. For further exploits of the Green Baron (as he was later nicknamed from his complexion) see the greatest aeroplane movie of all time – *Those Magnificent Men in Their Flying Machines.*

From then on the rot seems to have set in. Pilots have proceeded to torture themselves and their aeroplanes to the point of insanity (yes, even that). Wings folding up, propellers flying off, involuntary encounters with mother earth are all sadly part of aerobatics over the intervening years. Aircraft designers like Sukhoi have built machines that are virtually unbreakable – the pilot is going to 'break' before the plane. For what purpose? Well, let's not be too cynical, aerobatics can be graceful, entertaining and interesting for the REAL enthusiast when viewed in small doses, from a distance. Most enthusiasts will gladly look over the cockpit of the latest Sukhoi, Yak, Extra or Pitts, but you won't see them within a mile of a two-seat version with a pilot keen to offer a trip.

Air Britain

This is the grandfather of all the enthusiast organisations in the UK. Founded back in 1948 by Messrs Cain and Abel, it has attracted into its fold most of the aspiring REAL enthusiasts that could manage to part with more than their total week's pocket money. They didn't mind doing this, as they were able to sell the 'gen' on to the poor unfortunates who couldn't raise the ante to become members. Hence the development of an extensive network of Air Britain Branches all paying their 'dues' to support the international brotherhood.

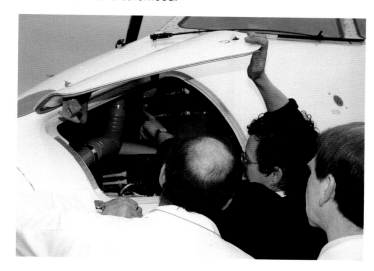

'Aha – that's where the constructor's number is.' BRIAN STRICKLAND

Within Air Britain there are a number of secret groups each totally dedicated to a specific aspect of aviation. Recently such topics have been discussed as: the colour of Saddam Hussein's underwear; the layout of the flight deck of the BAe 146 in which HRH The Prince of Wales had landing practice at Sumburgh, the fates of Bristol Fighters sold to Afghanistan; the colour and serial number of the Exocet missile decoy helicopter flown by HRH The Duke of York at the time of the Falklands War; why BAe did not fly the first FLA that it exhibited at Farnborough in 1994; who Westlands are going to con into buying the civil Heli-liner when the RAF didn't even want the EH101, and the aircraft movements list (landings only) for Boscombe Down in September 1994. They also publish the lively and exciting *Air Britain Digest*, with lots of lists of numbers that have been specially selected for regular readers.

'I'm not surprised his passengers want to get off.' PIERRE HOLLANDER

Air Correspondents

Not to be confused with Aviation Journalists (see later), Air (and Defence) Correspondents are employed by most National Newspapers and the Media (radio and TV), and profess to be experts in their field. This, as any enthusiast, REAL or even half witted, knows is one of the biggest jokes in this book. Most air correspondents, to judge by their reports, are quite incapable of differentiating between an aeroplane and a helicopter, or even a microlight and a hang glider. Mind you, since they appear to spend most of their waking hours as far away from their subject as they can – inside the airport terminal or in the Service Mess seeking out the bar, you shouldn't be too surprised.

'Look chaps the action's that way – it says BARred to the public.'
BRIAN STRICKLAND

Most people who read newspapers – or look at the pictures in the Sun and the Mirror as they are unable to read small print – might reasonably expect the main function of a newspaper to be that of disseminating news. In fact, this is a fallacy as all newspapers exist solely to invent and distort news. This is aided and abetted by the reporters and correspondents who specialise in air and defence matters. Their main job is concerned with scaremongering. That is why they spend most of their time writing stories like, 'Airbus computers set to fail every 3000 flights', 'Is air transport really safe?'; 'Are our defences up to the job?'; 'Are foreign airports potential death traps?'; 'Why are we giving away our Tornados to the Italians (or is it the Mafia)?'; 'Is low-flying training really necessary?' and 'Can we trust pilots?'

This, of course, is unfortunate, so it is probably just as well that most air and defence correspondents seem determined to pickle themselves from the inside out, since that clearly cuts down the amount of time that they can devote to actually dreaming up and writing stories that are specifically intended to frighten the public. However, there are exceptions! At times of international strife, otherwise known as 'when the Adie goes up', the defence correspondents spring into action. The Ministry of Defence, in its infinite wisdom, only permits Kate Adie (followed hotly by the rest of the media pack) to go to the trouble spots where the British Forces are involved. The MoD knows that it can rely on the defence correspondents to make up their reports from Kate's utterings, gleaned from the PR liaison officer or CNN's graphic account of the missiles flying over the enemy headquarters (from which they are reporting) and landing ten miles away in the middle of a housing estate. The Air Correspondent's task now is still to hide the truth, but with the objective of reassuring the readers, viewers and listeners how well our boys (and girls) are doing with the splendid equipment, that they (should) have with them but have left behind because we don't have any aircraft big enough to carry it.

Air Traffic Control

An organisation which exists to ensure that the sky is a safe place in which to fly. In the normal course of events the air traffic controllers use radar to monitor air traffic passing through the sky and radio to talk to pilots and tell them where to go, in a nice, polite way of course. They also control the traffic on the ground – planes, cars, lorries, buses, or cyclists, whatever moves on an airfield. Some of these air traffic controllers lead a troglodytic existence and see daylight only rarely. As a result, they can be easily recognised by their bleached complexions and dark glasses (even when it is raining). Others live in buildings with glass roofs, normally used for growing tomatoes – they all have beards and long hair. Air traffic controllers also have the highest divorce rate of any profession. Some say this results from the stresses and strains of the job, but the real reason is that they have some terribly anti-social and secretive habits. Many of them cannot give up their natural instincts for controlling everything that moves within their sight. There is also a significant number of REAL aviation enthusiasts amongst their number, who work, eat, sleep and play with planes and can only communicate in the quaint ATC language of alphas, holds, line-ups and controlled approaches.

'Not much on at the moment. Aerobatic team on final approach to land... C-130 on the runway with a burst tyre... a Hunter in the overhead carrying out a practice flame out... six US Army helicopters uncertain of their position and the Air Chief Marshal needs to depart three minutes ago.'

Airlines

Organisations, usually of a commercial nature, that fly fee-paying passengers from one point to another, in the (usually forlorn) hope of making a profit from this enterprise. Some enthusiasts spend their whole existence studying the fleets of airliners that scurry around the world. They fill whole magazines, every month, with the registration letters and flight numbers of airliners that grace the major airports of the world. These are SURREAL enthusiasts and fall outside the scope of this book.

'The nice thing about this new Airbus is that you don't have any flying controls. I even close my eyes when we land – it's all a bit frightening really.' PRM

Most enthusiasts have (usually reluctantly) to make use of airlines to visit aviation havens overseas, or to take an occasional busman's holiday. They have their own opinions (and names) for the world's leading (?) airlines. Here are just some of the printable ones:

British Airways – used to fly the flag with its all-Boeing fleet but now has decided to buy some Airbuses so has stopped flying the flag. One assumes that it is now carrying passengers instead. Before some clever dick at BA takes the REAL enthusiast to task – it did not buy the Airbus A320s – it inherited them from British Caledonian!

Virgin never takes you for a ride, but provides good value in getting funds from BA and a constant source of comment in the tabloids.

Aer Fungus – has recently announced that it has stopped providing hot meals on its flights to London from Dublin, now that it is making a profit on the route, but it will be providing two hot meals on the return journey, as it is cheaper to buy them at Heathrow. They are also going to re-introduce seats for all passengers in the cabin after the stewardess complained that she could not provide meals for the ten passengers and pilots on the flight deck of the Commuter Fokker 50 en route to Bristol recently.

Aeroplot – the former Soviet monopoly airline is now just a shadow of its old self. Gone are the luxurious standing room only, bring your own packed lunch flights to outlandish places. Instead, we now have luxurious two-to-a-seat, go when we please (or if the Moscow Mafia lets us), landing fees extra, flights to far off places that you could have reached last week, if you had been warned.

Air France – that other Concorde airline that still hasn't learnt how to operate the supersonic airliner, or any other of its aircraft profitably, probably because it is still run by the trade unions. Whatever British Airways does, Air France chooses the opposite way, so perhaps a time will come when they meet head on. Bet the European Union turns to Germany for the solution.

Lufthansa – still Europe's most regimented airline, probably due to the background of its long-serving staff, but unlike British Airways has a majority of Airbuses in its fleet. This is probably because they could insist on having corrugated skinning in the cargo hold and bars on the windows.

Cathay Pacific – or as it is better known Rafay Pacific, is entirely staffed by former RAF aircrew. Most have come from VC10, Hercules or Tristar backgrounds, but the occasional Tornado refugee can be instantly recognised by his unwillingness to fly above 15,000ft, and failure to believe that the weather radar is actually working.

Airships

Once thought to be extinct, multi-coloured airships are becoming increasingly common in British skies as mobile advertising hoardings. They are just about as boring as their static counterparts and have little interest to the REAL aviation enthusiast. There is perhaps just one sensible use for an airship, that is to carry TV cameras and cameramen aloft at major sporting events like Wimbledon or the Grand Prix at Silverstone. This is valuable on two counts – first in providing aerial close-ups of the sporting action (and into Damon Hill's car to see what he is doing when he waits for the starting flag to drop) and more importantly getting the darned TV cameramen out of the way when you as a spectator want to see what is happening.

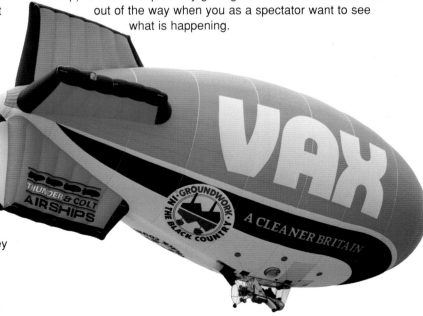

'The ruddy bag just got bigger 'n bigger, and the next moment we were off the ground.' PRM

Armed Forces

You might be surprised to learn that we spend more time at present trying to cut our strength by making qualified and experienced personnel redundant at great expense, and trying to give away, or loan our front-line aircraft, ships and tanks, than looking for ways to defend this country more effectively from the considerable number of new (and not so new) threats that are building up around the world. The REAL aviation enthusiast is acutely aware of this – but nobody listens, or if they do they don't want to hear.

Britain's armed forces comprise four services – the Army, the Royal Navy, the Royal Marines and the Royal Air Force. They all have air elements, and to be perverse and not very efficient, they all duplicate at least one of the other's military functions. The Royal Marines are (so we are led to believe) naval soldiers, some of which fly helicopters.

The Army has a special corps that is primarily equipped with helicopters, although it does have a limited number of fixed-wing aeroplanes. This special Corps is known as the Army Air Corps, which is indicative of a lack of imagination somewhere in the Army hierarchy. Army aviators are most easily recognised by their rather fetching blue berets. That isn't all they wear, of course, for they have boots and camouflaged battledress as well. Army aviators spend a lot of time flying their helicopters very slowly and very close to the ground. The reason why they do this is that they are unable to afford proper maps – in consequence, the only way they stand a reasonable chance of reaching the right destination is to stay low and follow the road signs.

The Royal Navy's Fleet Air Arm hasn't been the same since the end of the 'rum ration', after which naval aviators sobered up enough to realise that flying single- and two-seat aircraft above vast expanses of water wasn't exactly the sanest or safest way to make a living. For a start, there are no road signs to help them find their way home, although one smart Sea Harrier pilot did drop in on a container ship uninvited, to ask the way home. Naval aviators are most easily recognised by the fact that they wear funny trousers.

The Royal Marines can best be summed up with the phrase 'neither fish nor fowl', in that they aren't exactly soldiers, nor are they really sailors. The most accurate statement one can make is that they fall somewhere between the two extremes, insofar as they seem to like firing guns and making loud noises, while also deriving great enjoyment from messing about in dinghies. Some people say they can even walk on water. Whatever it is they do, it must be quite important, since they've been able to get away with stealing some Lynx and Gazelle helicopters from the Army Air Corps.

The Royal Air Force is of course the major operator of military aircraft and helicopters in Britain and devotes prodigious amounts of energy to frightening sheep, hikers, fell-walkers and other sorts of animal in Wales, the Lake District and Scotland. RAF aviators can be divided into two categories – pilots and navigators. Pilots sit in the front, so that they can see where they are going. Navigators, who really need to be able to see where they are going, so that they can tell where they are, sit in the back and see where they've been. Navigators are easily recognised, since they all wear puzzled expressions, almost as if they are wondering how they got to be where they are.

Aviation Archaeology

This is a fairly recent development – the aviation archaeologist coming along with the advent of the metal detector. Members will go to endless lengths, and in fact depths, to extract unrecognisable bits of twisted and scorched aluminium and other trivia from deep holes where aircraft are believed to have lost their struggle against gravity, for whatever reason.

A by-product is sometimes the establishment of some form of museum, quite often a shed in a garden, in which the various relics recovered are put on display. The successful groups do a roaring trade with others in supplying parts they do not need or that are surplus. As a result of these activities there is hardly an aviation museum in the country that does not own a part of the Dornier Do 17Z of Hauptmann Roth of KG76 that was shot down near Biggin Hill in the Battle of Britain, and is known as the 'Leaves Green Dornier'. If all these parts were re-assembled there would be enough to recreate the whole of KG76.

There is some danger involved in this type of work, as what is often not recorded is that after a recent excavation in Norfolk of a B-24, it was found that the electrics still worked; these were connected to a battery and blew the whole lot sky high as the bomb load was also still aboard. A search is going on for five enthusiasts, a JCB and two innocent bystanders. But the explosion, which also killed 5,000 turkeys, had its compensations when Bernard Matthews put £10,000 up front to fund a similar search.

IT'S SO UNFAIR! WE CHAPS IN THE SENIOR SERVICE SPEND OUR LIVES MILES OUT ON THE ATLANTIC; WHAT'S LEFT OF THE ARMY DISAPPEARS UNDER CAMOUFLAGE; THE ROYAL AIR FORCE IS SO DAMNED VISUAL!

Balloons

Montgolfier has an awful lot to answer for. You have a heavy night, a troubled sleep, wake to another frenetic day, get in your car to join the long commuting queues – and what do you get? A Branson look-a-like cheerily calls down to you out of the sky with 'good morning' or some other obscenity. He's suspended in a laundry basket below an overblown condom or some other equally outrageous shape, and every now and again lights an oversized bunsen burner that squirts out a huge column of flame. He's drifting aimlessly along in the wind without the slightest degree of control over where he's going. Altogether very nice if you can get it. But the rest of us have more to do than drift in the wind, scaring fellow humans outrageously early in the morning, and upsetting the farming community to boot. Yes, it might have been the earliest form of air travel, especially for animals, but that doesn't impress us poor mortals who have do a day's work to earn a crust.

'Now Miss Piggy, it's not just round the collar that you're going to feel the heat.' PAUL GINGELL

On reflection, perhaps it is a Scottish plot to de-stabilise the UK. Most of these modern-day outsize bin-liners are produced by Scotsman Don Cameron in Bristol, from whence he is sending them all over England. However, once a year (in August) he gathers as many as he can together near to his headquarters for what he calls the Bristol International Balloon Fiesta. This is something akin to the Godfather calling in the family to brief them on the plans for the coming year.

Perhaps a letter should be sent to British Aerospace pointing out that there is a busy aviation-related production facility in Bristol that could be purchased using the available funds from the sale of Rover Cars to BMW. That should ensure the closure of the balloon factory and its sale to the Taiwan Toy Balloon Company, or even the London Rubber Company (Bangkok Ltd) within a very short space of time. QED.

'Don't you feel a bit vulnerable udder 'ere?' PAUL GINGELL

BARG

Nothing to do with plotting the movement of longboats on Britain's canal system, but the acronym for the British Aviation Research Group – this country's best informed military aviation spy group. The Dutch would scramble to contest this, but as their magazine is written in an undecipherable language we cannot judge it. Suffice to say that BARG produces a monthly magazine (British Aviation Review) filled with the numbers of military aircraft, reported back to headquarters by its travelling members. As barely one-fifth is devoted to the UK's diminishing air arms, this title is somewhat inappropriate. However, since the rest reviews almost every other country in the world with armed aircraft, especially the USA, it is understandable why the leading subscribers have addresses in London W & SW1.

'It's a never ending job keeping up with these crafty pilots'. PETER COOPER

The Ministry of Defence uses it to keep track of the aeroplanes it owns, as it cannot always rely on the information that the pilots, squadron and base commanders supply. It is alleged that this has resulted in the ending of the sub-chartering of Tristars to UK airlines in the summer (when they were supposed to be down in the Falklands, or somewhere else a long way away; the profitable hiring of BAe 125s to a biz-jet company based near Stratford on Avon; the conclusion of a happy friendship between an Army Air Corps unit at Hereford and a helicopter hire company near London, who used to hire Agusta 109s to wealthy American tourists who liked their attractive yellow paint schemes and the use by various police forces of a couple of grey Islanders for following the movements of 'travellers' and visitors to pop festivals. The sudden movement of hordes of Fleet Air Arm helicopters to all parts of the UK and the near Continent in August, as recorded in BAR, came as a great surprise to their lordships, as they were under the misapprehension that the whole of the FAA went on annual leave in that month, and nothing moved. You will have noticed the reduction in Hercules movements on night mail flights, in and out of provincial airports.

BBMF

The Battle of Britain Memorial Flight (better known by its initials) is another of those RAF Strike Command reserve squadrons based at Coningsby. It is manned by the cream of British fighter pilots – the RAF's most highly qualified and experienced instructors in air defence and close combat flying. They fly a fleet of Spitfires and Hurricanes (only one of the latter at present, as the second aircraft is undergoing a highly secret 'stealth' rebuild and modification programme somewhere in Essex, after being shot down by a laser weapon over Wittering). These instructors are secretly training the pilots of the 20 or so Spitfires and Hurricanes currently dispersed around the UK, at places like IWM Duxford, ready for them to come together with their aircraft to re-establish the UK's air defence programme, when we finally pull out of the European Union. At this auspicious time the RAF will have made the final payment to the German and Italian Air Forces to take the last of its Tornado F3s, following the deferment of the Eurofighter 2050 programme until the computer boffins have removed the virus that keeps on telling it that it is a Harrier that can take off vertically.

The BBMF's other aircraft (which of course did not take part in that famous aerial confrontation), the Lancaster and Dakota, are flown by top RAF pilots who are awaiting a similar 'call to arms' by Strike Command. The Lancaster is being held as a contingency for the not too distant time when the remnants of the Tornado GR1 fleet are sold to Middle and Far East Air Forces to raise the necessary funds to build new headquarters for the three RAF Commands – and houses for its senior officers on the South Downs. The Dakota will be joined by a fleet of similar machines from Air Atlantique (Britain's equivalent of Air America), in 2005, to replace the last of the worn out C-130K Hercules with the RAF's transport fleet at Lyneham. They were expecting the BAe/Airbus internationally produced FLA (yes that F....ing Large Airfix machine shown at Farnborough in 1994) as a replacement by that date, but the planners, in their infinite wisdom, have drawn up this more realistic alternative.

'Pity they've had to put the Lanc back into service, now we've run out of GR1s. It's not the same displaying with this clapped out C-130K.' DANIEL MARCH

Biggles

Biggles look-alikes waiting to audition for the starring role in the latest blockbuster Those Magnificent Machines and their Flying Men (and Women). PRM

How is it that the author of every schoolboy's (and schoolgirl's?) favourite flying hero should be CAPTAIN W.E.Johns and not Squadron Leader or Wing Commander W.E.Johns? Throughout the living memory of every REAL aviation enthusiast, Biggles looms large. He is the intrepid aviator, who is and probably ever will be, playing an active role on the aviation scene. In all of us there is a Biggles (or Bigglette), just waiting to break out.

Here are some of the forthcoming Biggles titles scheduled to burst onto our bookshelves in the coming months.

Biggles in Arabia	D. Storm
Biggles Bombs Hanoi	Dr Alfred Price
Biggles Bombs Hanoi Again	Dr Alfred Price
Biggles Meets Budgie	Amy Toelicker
Biggles Reaches for the Sky	Sir Darth Vader
Julius Biggles	Capt W E Shakespeare
Biggles Buys Hollywood	Jackie Collins
Biggles at Bedtime	Enid Blyton & Jackie Collins
The Battle of Biggles	M E V Spitfire
Biggles Over Dunkirk	Michael Bowyer
Biggles Over Normandy	Michael Bowyer
(and 16 further titles)	
The World Air Power Biggles	Dave Donald & Jon Lake
Biggles in Love	Jilly Cooper
Biggles Gets Hooked	Jilly Cooper
Biggles Flies the Spitfire	Peter Underhill
Biggles at Biggin Hill	Michael Bowyer
(and 17 further titles)	
ABC of Biggles Recognition	Ian Allan
Jane's all the World Like Biggles	Paul Jackson
Biggles Joins the SAS	Anon
Biggles Was a Teenage Werewolf	Barbara Cartland
Biggles In Orbit	Chew Ing Gum (translated from the Chinese)
Biggles Bites the Dust	Fun Eraldi Rector

.....and this is just this year's list!

Biplanes

All the early pioneers failed with monoplanes, Icarus being a classic example, so when Orville and Wilbur Wright succeeded in making the first heavier-than-air aeroplane fly, and it was a biplane, everyone decided they must be right – their surname also helped this conviction. The truth of the matter is that the Wrights were bicycle makers, so naturally opted for two wings as well as two wheels, but more importantly they were working along the same lines independently and when they decided to join forces didn't want to waste their completed work, so used both sets of wings. For nearly forty years aircraft designers thought only of biplanes, mainly because:

In open cockpit aircraft the top wing helped keep the pilot dry in wet weather, and cool in hot weather;

As motor cars carried a spare wheel, it was only logical that aeroplanes should carry a spare set of wings;

The gradual introduction of only one set of wings was helped by the Second World War because as production increased, the demand for wings increased. In order to produce more planes the aircraft factories were told to restrict wings to one pair per aircraft. The Germans probably lost the First World War by building too many Fokker Dr1 Triplanes.

The attempt by Lockheed to introduce aeroplanes with no wings (ie the F-104) was a failure, so the monoplane now rules supreme.

Grumman Ag-Cat – single place biplane for crop spraying and aerobatics! LINDA'S ALL-THE-WORLD'S AIRCRAFT

Blackbird

This high performance, high-flying, super reconnaissance aircraft epitomises, for the REAL enthusiast, the USAF in the 1970s and 1980s. Sleek, black and awesome, the SR-71 was every schoolboy's dream. When it gave its final display at Mildenhall it brought tears to the eyes of grown men. The Blackbird was redundant – retired to the dusty wastes of Arizona – its role taken over by satellites and the new, yet to be seen, Aurora. But why are we putting this all into the past tense? Wake-up, the inevitable has happened. The immortal Blackbird is rising from the dead. Three SR-71s have been revived, at great cost, to fly again on active duty. USAF colonels have dusted off their space-suits and fought for a place in the cockpit of these veterans. What has happened to the Aurora and the TR-3? Does this have anything to do with mysterious goings on

at night from places as far apart as northern Nevada and Boscombe Down? Answers in the forthcoming REAL Aviation Enthusiast III.

Books

The aviation enthusiast is particularly fortunate in that he is well catered for by the publishing world, with several thousand books on all aspects of flight and flying being produced annually. We have invited a number of noted individuals, from a variety of walks of life, to nominate their favourite aviation titles. How many of them do you have?

- **A Guide to Flying Fish (Magnus Pike)**
- **Build your own Space Rocket (Patrick Moore)**
- **Pot Roasting Piston Engines (Delia Smith)**
- **Great Hoaxes of the Air (Jeremy Beadle)**
- **Cooking in Afterburner (Delia Smith)**
- **High Ground Wrecks (Chris Bonington)**
- **Bring Back Hang Gliding (Enoch Powell)**
- **The Hurricane Story (Michael Fish)**
- **Wind in the Willows (Michael Fish)**
- **Batting and the Boundary Layer (Geoffrey Boycott)**

British Aerospace

An aptly named company, famous for the open spaces it has created – Hatfield, Weybridge, Bitteswell, Kingston and so forth, and the famous names it has subsumed – Bristol, de Havilland, Hawker, Blackburn, English Electric, Scottish Aviation and Vickers, rather than any aircraft that it has solely created. Before you put pen to paper, as you surely will, to protest about this treatment of the great British institution that is normally reduced to two-and-a-half letters, recite your list of BAe designed and built aircraft. It will be over in a trice.

OK, there is just one redeeming feature, BAe has brought back Avro from oblivion. Well, if it can be done at Woodford for the 146 RJ Avrojet (and look what an immediate success that had in terms of orders), then why not give the Jetstream back to Scottish Aviation; the Harrier to Hawker; the Nimrod to Hawker Siddeley and the RAF's Eurofighters to English Electric (the English Electric EFA 2000 sounds really appropriate for a fly-by-wire, computer-controlled fighter). Oh, and let's call those 'new' tankers Vickers VC10 K4s.

CAA

More commonly known as the 'Conspiracy Against Aviators' or 'Consistently Against Aviation', this is the self-regulating body that controls all non-military flying activity in the UK. From its headquarters at Gatwick Airport it contrives, very successfully, to administer an Empire with laws, paperwork and taxes that would put Julius Caesar to shame.

The Civil Aviation Authority, to give it the official title, apparently has just one prime objective – that is to prevent any civil aircraft and/or aviator from getting into the air, until they have paid a large proportion of their income for what the CAA calls 'a privilege'. It continuously invents new rules and regulations (more recently seeking the assistance of its fellow brethren across Europe), to increase its income and thereby employ more staff to invent more rules *ad infinitum*. Its leader, who used to be one of the fastest men in Britain, is proud of the fact that he is accountable to no-one, apart from Parliament that gave him the first tablets of stone, to go forth and multiply.

As aviation enthusiasts have found to their cost, the CAA's tentacles stretch everywhere, and include the control of airshows. All organisers of flying displays have to pay a levy to permit them to run an airshow for the CAA's poacher turned game-keeper inspectors to come and inspect. Of course, the cost of all this has to be passed on to the punter, who, if the European collaborators have their way, will be watching the flying display from the next county, searching the skies with their telescopes to catch glimpses of the *Red Arrows* giving their display not below 5,000ft.

Oh, if you want to complain, don't bother trying. There is no mechanism for receiving any form of criticism or objection, you just have to grin and bear it – and of course pay-up. But it's all for safety, of course.

Cameras

REAL aviation enthusiasts own at least one 35mm single-lens reflex (SLR) camera, usually manufactured in Japan by Canon, Minolta, Nikon or Pentax. The casual onlooker might be deluded into believing that this is because these are the best cameras. Whilst true, it is not the only reason for using SLR cameras. The real reason is that it is impossible to see anything through the viewfinder of an SLR if the lens cap is still in place. This virtually eliminates the likelihood that the aviation enthusiast will forget to remove the lens cap, before attempting to take a picture. Most have done it with an old non-SLR camera.

It's not just one camera that is vital – there must be at least four spare bodies with 20 interchangeable telephoto lenses. This means that a colour print, or colour slide film, can be instantly available in a body. It then just becomes a question of fitting the right lens, setting the correct speed and aperture, in a few seconds, as the action unfolds before you. This of course takes years of practice, and many missed opportunities occur. But do not despair as all the photographs with fuzzy edges now have a future ahead of them. The latest computer scanning techniques mean that any fuzzy photo can be sharpened and touched up until it is looking quite professional. In fact any old photo can be made to look really good – you can change serials and registrations, put it into other national markings, take it out of one background and put into another – the opportunities are boundless. If you want to avoid the hassle of actually going and taking a photo yourself you can 'capture' it on your computer from TV or video pictures, save it in digital form and then have it printed. The days of the photograph never lying are long gone – but putting PRM after 99% of photos is here to stay!

Getting back to the properly equipped REAL enthusiast, a step ladder is also necessary, so that if you are short you can

'Hey, I've spotted the USAF F-15, it's just coming to the end of its display over Brize.' BRIAN STRICKLAND

see over the heads of those in front of you at air displays, and if you are tall, you can take good pictures of the tops of aeroplanes. An aluminium case to carry films, filters, lenses, tripods, bipods and lens hoods is also essential, although its real purpose is for the display of stickers.

Major problems faced by enthusiasts wanting to use their valuable camera equipment at displays and other aviation venues are manifold. Here are just a few that they would like to get:

- display pilots to appreciate just how hard it is to photograph their aircraft if they go too fast.
- organisers to hold their displays in good weather.
- a position where the sun is in the right place all day when the organisers do manage a good day.
- the paying public to keep their heads out of tailpipes of jet aircraft, air intakes of all aircraft, posing against wings, tails, rockets, drop tanks and cockpit steps, whilst 'dad' records the happy event with his new mini-compact zoom that he doesn't know how to use.
- a Press Pass, to get into the best position to take photos of the visiting VIPS (I think not).

The financial rewards for all this time and effort are minuscule, but keep on trying – you might be another budding John Bidds or Duncan Cuboid and find there is more to aviation photography than just flashing your stickers.

Now the REAL enthusiast comes well prepared with a caravan to carry his ladder. Useful to find out which way the wind's blowing too. PETER COOPER

Civil Aviation

This is a branch of flying that the majority of people are familiar with, since they come face to face with it when they go on holiday or on business trips. It attracts a totally different type of REAL enthusiast from those into military aviation. They range from those who spend every waking moment in the public viewing area of the nearest 'international' airport (yes they are ALL prefixed international now, even the tiny strip in Wales with one flight a week to England), to those who are well heeled enough to spend every waking moment at the Club (flying of course), flying or talking about Cessnas, Pipers and various

'So that's why they collect civil registrations.' DANIEL MARCH

extinct tribes of American Indians (most popular American light civil aircraft are named after these).

One of the unsolved mysteries surrounding the civil aviation enthusiast is why so many of them collect fiction in the form of airline timetables and aircraft registration letters, or put adverts like this in magazines like *Aviation News*: 'Can anyone help Salford spotter with reggie of unknown airliner that flew over Manchester at 45,300ft at 13.13hr on Sunday 29 February 1992?'

The places where numbers of civil enthusiasts congregate together is quite limited and is confined almost exclusively to cafeteria areas at major international airports such as Heathrow, Gatwick, Glasgow, Manchester and Birmingham. They can also be observed from time to time at Bristol, East Midlands, and Newcastle Airports, but that probably has more to do with the accident of where they live rather than anything else.

Many are afflicted by a particularly severe form of dyslexia, as a cursory glance at a civil enthusiast's log-book will soon confirm. It will be filled with a mixture of odd hieroglyphics, epitomised here by a sample entry extracted at random with minimum force from an individual at Heathrow (be advised that log-books are highly treasured artifacts and that their contents are guarded jealously).

28/9/92 D-AIAN SX-BEB HB-IPC TC-JCA G-BKYI OO-SDL VT-EFJ HZ-AIG

It obviously means something, but since it is quite clearly written in code, a mainframe computer would almost certainly be required to establish the significance of this entry. Approaches to GCHQ at Cheltenham for assistance in deciphering the above (and other similar entries) met only with stony silence.

REAL civil aviation enthusiasts can be spotted because they will all have:

- a pair of binoculars around their neck;
- at least 23 pencils and five notebooks in a tatty sports bag;
- a very tatty copy of *Civil Aircraft Markings*
- their necks at a constant angle of 45deg to the horizon.

Their ambitions will include a wish to:

- receive an erotic note from an Aeroflot stewardess on a package trip to Siberia;
- buy a house 100m from the threshold of Runway 28L at Heathrow
- become eccentric enough to join the ranks of REAL military aviation enthusiasts.

Clothing

Since publication of our first dissertation on the REAL enthusiast's standards of dress, there has been a £200,000 in-depth study by the RAF Benevolent Fund Enterprises for the BBC's popular Clothes Show. Its totally irrelevant report, which was the main feature in the Clothes Show Live programme from Birmingham International Airport last winter, is published here in full. It begins with the revealing statement that the aviation enthusiast is completely lacking in any form of dress sense whatsoever, and can therefore be observed in any and all sorts of clothing. About the only thing that can be stated about the enthusiast's clothing, with any degree of certainty, is that it will not be colour co-ordinated. Nevertheless it has discovered that for the REAL aviation enthusiast clothing is important, and it also provides clues as to the level of enthusiasm of the wearer.

The report goes on to point out that there are five different classifications of avialogist – the 'Dabbler'; the 'Keen'; the 'Avid'; the 'Fanatic' and the 'Obsessive'. Each may easily be distinguished by a close study of clothing. All but the first can be prefixed REAL.

There is no difficulty for female enthusiasts in America to show that they are REAL. Eye and head shades are essential.

The remainder of the report can best be summarised as utter rubbish. So, next time you visit your local international airport, or sit in the enthusiasts' enclosure at a major airshow, why don't you make your own assessment of the inmates and their clothing. You might be able to sell your report to Sky News to fill in another half hour of mindless chatter.

Concorde

Don't ask the Tornado F3 pilot what happened when the RAF chartered a British Airways Concorde for interception trials around the UK, because it's top secret. But we can tell you what the BA pilot said when asked the same question – Concorde always got away unscathed.

Concorde is set to remain the world's fastest airliner well into the next century. That infamous Financial Times columnist Mary Gasring must still be suffering acute indigestion from eating so many of her hats. Concorde's popularity never wanes with the public. Advertise a supersonic charter into your local airport and it will be fully booked in a very short time. When the airliner arrives the whole area will be thronged with gawpers brandishing their Jessop's compacts, all striving to produce a photograph of Concorde landing. But, of course, all they will get is a shot of a delta-winged fly in the middle (if they're lucky) of a huge area of sky. Auntie Bertha's hat in the bottom right hand corner looks quite artistic.

REAL enthusiasts know that the best place to photograph Concorde is at Heathrow, at least three times a day on a scheduled arrival, or on the annual visit back to its ancestral seat at Fairford for IAT. They also know that there is a growing movement to reclaim the supersonic airliner's name to the English language. After all it is British Airways and not Air France that has made a resounding success of its operation in commercial terms. Mon général is no more, Mrs Thatcher told them where to get off, so why shouldn't it be proudly British CONCORD?

In our first edition we introduced you to Dick the REAL enthusiast and what he was wearing in 1987. This same Dick is shown here eight years later, showing how his clothes have matured with age.

PETER COOPER

Confederates

Although they would never admit to it, a number of British enthusiasts have been seen mingling with their US counterparts on more than one occasion in Texas. They have responded to the call from the Confederate Air Force at Midland to attend their annual airsho (no, it's not another mistake – just the way that these strange southerners spell it). This splendid organisation brings together a unique collection of mainly WW2 survivors – planes and pilots – every October. Everyone who joins the CAF becomes a full colonel (there are no other ranks), but of course this is the last thing that a British enthusiast will do. He takes great delight in watching his American friends playing at being in the military and being distracted from the main objective of being there. If you ever have the urge to attend with your family, you will find that Midland is probably one of the most boring and uninteresting places (apart from the aircraft) in the whole of the USA. It is 3,000ft up on a windy plateau, verging on the desert. It's the sort of place where you would send your younger brother for a six months holiday after he has just taped over your only copy of *Those Magnificent Men in Their Flying Machines* or forgotten to give you the telephone message that you have a tour of the US aircraft carrier *John F Kennedy* arranged for five minutes ago and 50 miles away.

'Must just pop back for the instruction manual. I'll get it right next time.' PRM

down the narrow country lanes. It also has a longer term effect of moving the crowd line further away from the displaying aircraft (which means he has to buy a yet longer and still more expensive lens for his camera); higher insurance and other costs for the organiser, which means that the admission price goes up next year and worst of all the air correspondents bring their doom and gloom to bear in the nationals, suggesting that all airshows are dangerous and should be banned. No, aircraft crashes are not popular with enthusiasts, unless they happened a very long time ago and some interesting aircraft is now being recovered from its crash site.

'By golly that little chap's got his finger on the button. (Red Arrows in Texas – lady making a proposal that Les Garside Beattie couldn't possibly refuse.) PRM

Crashes

Aircraft accidents are not at all popular with aviation enthusiasts. In fact, like most pilots, REAL enthusiasts find them inconvenient and unhelpful. When an accident occurs at an airshow it disrupts or even stops the flying, causes the roads to be blocked and prevents him from leaving early (usually when the *Red Arrows* are displaying) to beat the madding crowds

'Next time I'll build it with fixed wings.' PRM

Desert Storm

This was sparked off by Saddam Hussein's wish to own all those Q8 filling stations around Britain that were offering free glasses in exchange for buying 80 gallons of petrol. The Iraqi leader had mis-read the advertisements (because he is short-sighted, from spending so long in his underground bunkers doing naughty things) and thought that they were spectacles on offer. He had stopped the manufacture of glasses in Iraq as it was using up too much of the sand that he needed to build his new castle outside of Baghdad. He planned to obtain all the Q8 glasses and sell them to his Army, so that they could read their maps in future and find their way back to base after a quick attack on the Marsh Arabs or the Kurds. There was a basic flaw in his wicked plot, that even the lowliest aviation enthusiast would have spotted – after getting mastery of Q8 how would he get his hands on the glasses? Of course, the Americans helped him out before he even realised that there was a flaw. They challenged him to a war and if he accepted they would bring in the British, French and Italians – to name a few, with their glasses to boot. They called the war *Desert Storm* although the fiercely independent British insisted on giving it their own inappropriate name Operation *Granby*.

For the REAL aviation enthusiast this was a time of great excitement. Stories from the front line of sand painted Tornados and Jaguars with lurid paintings on their noses filtered back home. Soon there was a pink Tristar, then a Hercules or two (but we cannot talk about these). Chinooks sprouted door-mounted guns and had speckled paint-work (for night-flying trials according to an MoD spokesman – for special forces flying the SAS deep into Iraq said the notice board in front of one of these helicopters at an airshow). And so it went on – Saddam Hussein never got his glasses, but neither did he get the come-uppance he deserved. The RAF came home somewhat wiser than before and the enthusiasts had a field day photographing the exotic paint schemes on the *Granby* aircraft.

Granby identified new operational skills to the RAF. PRM

Designations

A subject dear to the hearts of most enthusiasts, the multiplicity of aviation designations, acronyms, mnemonics, nicknames, definitions, slang and jargon is covered several times in this book. Mastery of this, sometimes difficult, subject is essential for the REAL enthusiast. So let's just introduce it gently here with a short initial guide.

Ass first	Canard aircraft = Viggen
Aluminium overcast	Delta-bomber = Vulcan
Blue Circle	Swinger = Tornado F2
Buff	Big Ugly Fat Fella = B-52
Cab	Army chopper = helicopter
Delta	Don't ever land there again
Dragon Lady	Deuce = Lockheed U-2
Fat Albert	Herky Bird = C-130 Hercules
Fred	Flaming Ridiculous Economic Disaster = C-5 Galaxy
Gooney Bird	Puffship = C-47 Dakota
Huey	Cobra = Bell UH/AH-1
MRCA	Must Refurbish the Canberra Again = Tornado
QANTAS	Quite a Nice Touch-Down. Any Survivors?
SLUF	Short Little Ugly Fella = A-7 Corsair
Thud	Lead Sled = F-105 Thunderchief
Wild Weasel	HARMless = F-4G Phantom
Wokka Wokka	Shithook = CH-47 Chinook

Ejection Seats

These handy 'get-you-home-safe' devices are only ever fitted in military aircraft and are meant as a last resort device for use by aircrew, who have no other option but to abandon their aircraft. Contemporary ejection seats rely on rocket motors to propel them and their occupants clear of the aircraft in which they are installed as a prelude to making a safe descent by parachute. They are all manufactured by Martin-Baker, although a referral to the Monopolies Commission by Avalon Quality Seating (as supplied to No 10 Downing Street) is pending at the moment.

Individuals who have had to use ejection seats are members of a very select club. In recognition of the fact, they are given a special tie by Martin Baker, it being widely accepted that this is cheaper than letting them keep the seat, which the manufacturer insists should be returned after use for re-cycling. Next time you ride on a Martin Baker mountain bike, spare a thought for the person who last occupied a somewhat larger version of your seat.

Since the sudden acceleration involved in the use of an ejection seat can often result in chronic back trouble, it would be somewhat more appropriate to give the ejectees a bunch of gift vouchers that can be redeemed at one of the chain of Martin Baker chiropractors, located in all the major cities near to military airfields.

Incidentally, if you visit Martin Baker's airfield at Chalgrove you might see the company's dayglo and silver Meteor taking to the air. Now in its 45th year of flying, the company is determined to get the first seat that it fitted to this aircraft to work properly, as they want to recover the chief test engineer's false teeth that dropped beneath the seat pan when he leant forward to do up the dummy's straps on a freezing cold December's day in 1950. They want to refute the theory that the seat is hanging on by the skin of his teeth.

'That man from MB was here for the seat before the pilot reached terra firma.' BRIAN STRICKLAND

Enthusiasts

Enthusiasts come in all shapes and sizes – some form themselves, into 'spotters' societies' and 'fliers' flocks.' LINDSAY PEACOCK

The world of aviation is little different from other areas of human activity in that it arouses the intense interest of a disparate bunch of individuals who can best be described as devotees or, perhaps even more appropriate, as acolytes. If we consult an awfully good dictionary, we learn that the definition of acolytes actually stipulates that these are members of an inferior order, who serve the superior orders in the 'ministry'. The key word in this definition is 'inferior'. Let no one be in the slightest doubt that aviation enthusiasts are viewed as inferior beings by all non-aviation enthusiasts, and particularly so by anyone who happens to be employed by the national press or the BBC.

Aviation enthusiasts come in all sorts of shapes and sizes. There are thin ones, fat ones (sorry, gravitationally-challenged ones – let's conform to politically acceptable terminology shall we?), tall ones (vertically-disadvantaged ones), shy ones, brash ones, retiring ones and retired ones. About the only thing they have in common is that they are all differently normal.

Collectively, they are several thousand sandwiches short of the full picnic. Would anyone in their right mind, and full possession of their mental faculties, spend several hours tramping around in knee-deep grass on a rain-swept airfield, in the teeth of a howling gale, in order to gawp at large and inanimate metal objects?

Aviation enthusiasts form themselves into groups, societies, clubs and organisations, most of which reflect in their names the particular field in which they are interested, as well as the subject they cater for. Some are called spotters, but this has nothing to do with their skin condition.

Events

The aviation enthusiast is certainly not starved of opportunities to indulge his (or her) passion for watching flying objects during the summer months, since every weekend from May to September will feature several events with an aeronautical flavour. Be warned, however, that the scope of some of these events can vary quite alarmingly – and that some may only feature a token aviation involvement, which is highly unlikely to give complete satisfaction to the REAL enthusiast. As a general rule any event which features the word 'air' in its title is usually likely to include some aeronautical involvement.

REAL air events are frequently held on days that are either wet, windy, showery or very, very hot. Sometimes it is a combination of all of these. This is to allow the organiser the chance of giving raincoat, umbrella, sun-hat, tee-shirt, arctic survival gear, sun-glasses, hot-dog, ice-cream and coffee vendors equal opportunity of paying him a large sum of money to fleece the desperate enthusiast. Listen to the commentator on a hot, sunny day telling everyone to cover their heads. So they trot off to the nearest stall and buy a baseball hat for £6 (the same one that was on sale at their local Sunday market last week for £3).

Organisers of air events put a great deal of thought into the location of the event. The bigger it is, the more care has to be given to making sure that it is accessed only by narrow country lanes, that the local community is aware of the event, so that the cows are brought in from the fields along the lanes just after 10.00am. Deliveries of straw, to be placed in the car parks, to help bogged down cars extricate themselves are arranged for the middle part of the day, after the combine harvesters have gone back along the lanes to the farm so that the farmer can watch the display from the comfort (and shelter) of his farmhouse. There are other considerations too – the date should be arranged to coincide with another different event (such as a horse race meeting, car rally or tennis tournament) so that visitors coming to the area have a choice while they are sitting in their stationary car, some 20 miles distant.

There is now such a proliferation of titles used for air

"C-5 Galaxy Club": Members Meet.

'Call this an air race, it's more like the M-25 at 5.00pm on a Friday.'
ANDREW MARCH

events, the following survey is intended to provide readers with a shrewd idea of what to expect, as well as which of these types of event might be worth attending. It is not a comprehensive guide, and at the end of the day you 'pays your money and takes your choice'...

Air Day – Can mean anything the organiser wishes it to mean. May involve several hundred aircraft, but probably won't. Might include flying activity – but probably won't. Be warned that air days are never cheap and do remember to take an umbrella because it is bound to rain.

Air Display – Weather permitting, this type of event will include flying activity of some kind, but it might be limited to a hot air balloon being inflated or a helicopter hopping up and down a few times. Be warned that air displays are never cheap – and do remember to take an umbrella, because it is bound to rain.

Air Extravaganza – A good rule of thumb to use, when considering if an event will be worth attending, is to count the number of letters in the title of the event in question. Experience has shown that the more letters there are, the worse the event is likely to be.

Air Fair – Despite the presence of the word air in the title, this will probably have little to do with aviation and nor will there be a fair so you won't be able to amuse yourself by knocking seven bells out of anyone else on the dodgems. There will be a car boot sale in a field somewhere, but there is unlikely to be anything worth buying. It will rain torrentially all day and your car will end up buried to the axles in mud.

Air Fête – Sort of like an Air Fair, only with a maypole and a bunch of people in silly clothes trying to avoid getting tangled up, while dancing around it with a load of streamers. It will rain torrentially all day, but you won't get stuck, since a steam traction engine meeting will also be taking place and one of those magnificent veteran machines will tow you out of the mire for a modest fee.

Air Pageant – An excuse for bringing out a load of old aeroplanes and getting them to taxi up and down a few times. It will be far too windy (according to the organiser and sole pilot) to fly any of the aeroplanes that day.

Air Race – As spectacles go, this is a complete waste of time. It will also be a hugely expensive waste of time. About the only thing you are likely to see will be a bunch of tiny dots in the distance – and you'll only recognise them if you're lucky, since the commentator's microphone is bound to break down at the crucial time, so you don't know who ends up winning, even if the organisers can decide.

Air Show – Still the most common classification of all, an air show can mean almost anything the organiser wants it to mean in terms of size and scale. As a result, the number of aircraft on display can vary enormously. This is your safest bet for seeing some REAL aeroplanes in the air, but you might have to pay dearly for the privilege.

Air Spectacular – Similar to an Air Extravaganza – but with three aircraft and, if you are really lucky, one or two helicopters. Air Spectaculars usually take place in Ireland, so it will probably be wet.

Air Tattoo – How anyone in their right mind could use this title for an airshow beggars belief. Perhaps they had in mind the thought that happy memories of long queues for the hidden loos, surviving ten hours of continuous jet flying, paying twice the going rate for an aviation magazine and being deluged as the heavens opened would be tattooed on the visitors minds, to encourage them to make the same sacrifices again the next year.

And of course, if the prefix International is used in the title it might mean that there is a visiting Cessna 172 from Jersey, if it is a civil event, or an F-16 from Belgium or Holland in the static display, if military.

Of course, not all airshows fit into the above generous categories. The REAL aviation enthusiast finds out before the last day for obtaining advance tickets at reduced prices, or stakes out the corner of the farmer's field with the best views of the landing approach and flying display.

The one advantage of air displays is that they sometimes provide aircraft to shelter under. DANIEL MARCH

Farnborough

From the cradle of British aviation as the Royal Aircraft Factory, to the leading aviation research and development centre – the Royal Aircraft Establishment, Farnborough is now just a biz-jet airfield under threat of closure and the pen-pusher's repository for British Aerospace. Oh yes, it does still host the biennial caterer's convention – the Society of British Air Caterer's Farnborough International, much loved by the National Free-lunchers Association, air and defence correspondents, Raymond Baxter and the entire staff of the BBC Television Centre, who take up residence throughout the week.

As an aviation enthusiast you could once upon a time be guaranteed a worthwhile day out at Farnborough for the airshow that was squeezed in between a late finishing lunch in the chalets and the foreign pilot's desire to get in a bit of shopping (or something else) in London before sun-down. Particularly on the public days at the weekend (by which time the pilots couldn't afford any more trips to London) you could be treated to an exciting airshow by many types of aircraft that you had never seen before (probably because they were new prototypes). They were augmented by set pieces – quite imaginatively presented by the three services. This was at a time when they had to recruit many new aircrew to train to fly the large number of aircraft with which they were defending our interests.

Where has that magic gone today? Probably down the road to Fairford or Biggin Hill. The trouble is there are no new airworthy prototypes to present; the armed forces are trying to give away their aircrew (230 pilots in 1995) and lease their aircraft to foreign air forces (Tornado F3s to Italy and GR1s to the Middle East); there are more regulations and unenthusiastic organisers who prefer to sit back contemplating past glories. Let's hope that the word Farnborough can really mean something again to the British air minded public (and the enthusiast of course) before it becomes just a faded memory of better times.

'No we won't hurry up – we're the newest prototype at Farnborough and the gullible British public have paid to see us.' PRM

FIAT

To the man, woman or even child in the street, FIAT is an Italian car manufacturer. One of this company's most noted creations in the automotive field was the Fiat 500, which could be called the first 'compact car'. Indeed, it was so compact that people of normal height were only able to drive it by poking their heads out through the sun roof. They tried it in the aerospace field too. The Fiat G-91 stands out head and shoulders as the world's only successful 'lightweight' (by comparison with other contemporary designs) jet fighter, being produced in reasonable quantities for Italy and Germany.

To the aviation enthusiast FIAT is an acronym standing for Friends of International Air Tattoo. It is not an organisation for the elite, insofar as anyone who can afford the fee can join. This naturally means that it attracts all sorts of people from all sorts of walks of life. So, FIAT members include the gamut of enthusiasts, ranging from the mildly interested right up to the so-called 'superspotter'. In the main they are a bunch of dedicated REAL enthusiasts, most of whom are members of every club, group or society mentioned in this book, but deserve their own separate entry, mainly because this book is published by the RAF Benevolent Fund, which receives the donations paid by FIAT members through their subscriptions (and from the sales of this book).

Members of FIAT come in all shapes, sizes, colours, creeds, and callings but all (or at least most) have the following in common: ... they run the gauntlet of a weekend at Fairford every July; all love travelling on open top buses; all have at least ten SLR 35mm cameras, eight lenses and a former U-boat commander's binoculars; all can recite the BARG participants at IAT shows lists for the last ten years, all love to be herded into an enclosure where they can stand for four days, talking, sleeping, living, and dreaming aviation – and if lucky sniffing Avtur or Avtag.

They are the only known human species totally feared by RAF Police dogs, either singularly or collectively... But they are the epitome of the REAL enthusiast and without them aviation probably wouldn't exist, at least not as we know it today. Inevitably, since membership is open to anyone who has the correct amount of money, the FIAT enclosure will also contain some riff-raff as well as a few nerds, one or two dweebs, at least three Mr Beans and a couple named Gerald and Cynthia, who thought they were buying tickets for the British Grand Prix from a well-known Italian car manufacturer, when they signed up.

FIAT Escape Committee

A mysterious and shadowy organisation, made up entirely of enthusiasts dedicated to discovering ways and means of breaking out of the FIAT enclosure. Their objective is to reach the various static aircraft parking areas on the Friday before the show weekend and the Monday after it. So far, they have only managed to accomplish this on one occasion, despite the committee including a pair of Dutch 'superspotters' who have succeeded in breaking into most of the Russian air bases in Germany. Their continued failure may, it is surmised, have something to do with the organiser's use of techniques taken from books and films, and the employment of that infamous former enthusiast BB (no, not the ex-French film-star with her dogs) as guard commander.

Thus far, the only attempt that has succeeded involved four individuals (two Dutchmen, a Brit and a Pole) who disguised themselves as workmen, uprooted a complete Portaloo and proceeded to carry it out of the compound before heading off towards the unbarriered part of the static display. But don't try that again this year, the organisers are wise to this bit of trickery and now lock the doors of all portable toilets in the FIAT enclosure during daylight hours.

FIAT enclosure guards pose for a photograph in front of the Russian Bear, knowing that all the members have gone home. Why? Look in the sky. PRM

Films

To the REAL aviation enthusiast, films are the next best thing to air shows, and the arrival of the video has made those long winter evenings much more bearable. If you have satellite or cable TV you well know all the flying films that have ever been made, as they are repeated endlessly. The important thing in all this is to be able to spot errors made during filming and quote these to fellow enthusiasts, or anybody who cares to listen. The cinema industry has devoted thousands of miles of film and spent vast amounts of money on the production of movies with an aeronautical theme. It is to be regretted that the film-makers' view of aviation has virtually nothing to do with reality, as anyone who has more than a casual interest will quickly realise. We venture to suggest that there is only one aviation film that meets all of an aviation enthusiast's enjoyment criteria and is therefore worth watching time and time again. This is *Those Magnificent Men in their Flying Machines* starring the late, great Terry Thomas and Tony Hancock.

The best – indeed, the only – way to approach any film that has a substantial aviation content is with scepticism, since the typical aviation buff is certain to spot errors. These can be a huge source of amusement, although do bear in mind the fact that serious cinema-goers are unlikely to be amused when you break into gales of hysterical laughter on seeing some glaring mistake. So don't watch *Top Gun* at your local cinema unless you are happy to be pursued by a mob of irate film buffs. So, a word of warning, if you are prone to fits of laughter while watching films with an aeronautical flavour, rent the videos so you can see them at home, and laugh to your heart's content.

These are just a few of the aviation classics with some of their more obvious howlers. You are beginning to qualify as a REAL enthusiast if you can find at least as many again when you watch the film for a second time.

The Dam Busters	Wrong radar aerials on Lancasters, Lincolns making up numbers in background
Battle of Britain	Two-seat Spitfire; Merlin engined Me-109s; Anson C19 in a background; Susannah Yorks' 1969 vintage suspenders.
The Blue Max	Tiger Moth, Stampe
Hell's Angels	Avro 504K, Boeing Stearman.
633 Squadron	Post-war Anson again; the wrong mark Mosquito,
Mosquito Squadron	The same Mosquitos; that dreaded Anson yet again.
Aces High	Inserts from *The Blue Max*.
Fighter Squadron	Luftwaffe pilot speaking German without American accent.

When you've sorted these out take a look at the following, and find even more howlers in: *Apocalypse-Now*, *The Great Waldo Pepper*, *A Gathering of Eagles*, *Memphis Belle* (not the wartime original) and *Top Gun*. Of course you won't mind the mistakes in *Hot Shots*, will you?

'OK Mr Puttnam, I will cut the blades down to the same size, but I'm sure it won't go as fast as that one.' PRM

Flight Refuelling

'Refuelling complete boss, kilo two three would like to know when you want to collect the 99 wine glasses.'

This is a means by which military aircraft transfer fuel from one aircraft to another whilst flying aimlessly around in circles over the North Sea, or on rare occasions extending the range of small aircraft like the Harrier to attend permanent airshows on the borders of Iraq, or hop across for a couple of weeks entertainment in Las Vegas. Enthusiasts are regularly treated to visits by air-to-air refuelling tankers (from the RAF and foreign air forces) at IAT Fairford for the all too frequent Skytanker Meets. There are several theories why these flying Texaco tankers are so popular with the organisers: the boss man has run out of lighter fuel; the organiser's Amstrad word processor used for sending out invitations ran out of memory when it had stored the addresses of all the tanker units around the world; the USAF wants to sell off its fuel to the departing tankers after the show as there is no more room at the filling station and tanker pilots want to have a proper look at some of the aircraft that they give fuel to.

Flight Refuelling used also to be the name of the company founded by Sir Alan Cobham, that invented air-to-air refuelling and has manufactured every probe and drogue system purchased by the RAF, and a number of overseas air arms. When it recently succeeded in swallowing up its only major rival in the world, the Sergeant Fletcher company in America, the company decided to drop its descriptive name and let everyone know who is now king, and renamed it Cobham. Perhaps we will see the same thing happening to other aerospace companies, engine manufacturers and even the names of air displays. Watch this space!

Follow Me Vehicles

Some of the bigger airshows like Biggin Hill and IAT, and some Spanish airports, such as Alicante, have special vehicles to guide visiting aircraft to their allotted parking spots on the airfield. The successful outcome of this is entirely dependent upon good radio communications, a clearly understood procedure and intelligent driver, or it simply becomes the blind leading the blind.

To get over the problem of persuading the pilot to actually

'Follow me, I'm lost too, but isn't it fun.' PRM

follow the vehicle sent to guide him in, one airshow decorated its follow-me vehicle in an enticing manner.

IAT had to introduce special follow me procedures for the visit of the first Russian Air Force Bear. A whole fleet of vehicles was deployed to cover every runway exit and taxi-way, as the crew could not speak English. They needn't have worried though, the Russians had a former Soviet Air Force map that clearly marked every inch of RAF Fairford and even gave the thickness of the surface over the entire paved area of the airfield.

Food

The dedicated enthusiast will refuel on almost anything. Usually, this is done in one gulp. If it isn't small enough to fit in the mouth, he or she will still eat it, but it may take a while longer, since very few aviation enthusiasts have shown much aptitude for the process of biting and chewing. PETER COOPER

Girls

A bit of a minefield this, in the age of political correctness. Since the first edition of this tome was produced we have seen great advances into what was very much a male dominated activity. Now we have a number of REAL female aviation enthusiasts, or so we are led to believe. There is even a lady (she won't thank me for using this term) editor of a new, vibrant aviation magazine. Again we have to thank BB for this occurrence, which some see as a natural progression in the genre's quest to subjugate the male's dominance of most interesting activities. Watch out fishermen, they are heading in your direction now!

The consensus of opinion amongst all three aviation enthusiasts who dared to voice an opinion on this subject, is that they are in support of more women and girls taking an interest in aviation. They make the following provisos, that they should never: expect men to carry their stepladders; refuse to buy their round in the pub; chatter loudly and make remarks like "Isn't this fun" when 50 yards inside the fence at a Russian air base; start complaining if they snag their tights on barbed wire, or get mud on their shoes while tramping across a field to reach the end of a runway...or begin moaning about the cold...and the wind...and the rain...or drone on and on at inordinate length about the mess that it's making of their hair, clothes or complexion.

Gliding

This is flying on the cheap, and mainly for those with plenty of time to hang about an airfield, helping to launch others into the air, waiting for their five minutes worth at the end of the day when there is no lift left to keep the glider airborne. No REAL aviation enthusiast, male or female, worth the title would engage in such a boring, pointless and time-wasting pursuit. They would much rather sit in the comfort of their local airport terminal waiting for the three-hour delayed Air Jamaica charter flight from Majorca, or sit in their car at the threshold of Lakenheath waiting for the next transit flight of Nighthawks reported to be coming sometime in the following week. After all, who in their right minds would knowingly and willingly commit themselves to the heavens in a flying machine that doesn't have an engine?

Great Mysteries of Flight

We have all heard the so called experts putting forth their theories on some of those unexplained mysteries of flight involving the disappearance of famous pilots and personalities like Amelia Earhart, Bert Hinkler, Glenn Miller, Henry Ford, Howard Hughes, Lord Lucan, the pilot who took off in a Piper from Compton Abbas and flew to his nadir on 1 May 1993 and dozens more. Or suggesting knowledgeably what is happening in the Bermuda Triangle?

The majority of aviation enthusiasts are not the least interested in these hypotheses, they have, as air travellers, much more important 'mysteries of flight' that they would like answered.

Great Mysteries I - Can you identify this military helicopter photographed at a secret European air base? TIM PRINCE

Great Mysteries II - How does the pilot of this aircraft at Hong Kong International Airport get all of these passengers on board? PRM Solutions on the next page.

Here are just a few further mysteries that urgently need solutions.

Why is it that no matter where you sit in an airliner, you are always the last to be served with a meal; and even more importantly the last to be reached with the drinks trolley, by which time only Diet Dishwater remains?

Why is it that you can be cruising along quite peacefully, without the slightest sign of turbulence, until they begin pouring out the tea or coffee, at which point all hell invariably seems to break loose and the aircraft begins bouncing about all over the place, and with it your drink?

Why is it that after waiting until bursting point for the 'toilet occupied' sign to go out, your route is completely blocked by a trolley loaded with duty free, over-priced booze and cigs?

Why do other passengers always leap to their feet and begin desperately pulling hand baggage out of the overhead racks as soon as the aircraft stops, even though they must know that they're going to end up standing in the aisle for at least seven minutes?

And why, (this is the greatest mystery of all) is my suitcase always the last to appear on the baggage carousel?

If you can help to explain some of these mysteries, you'll be doing me and all enthusiasts a real favour.

GREAT MYSTERIES SOLUTIONS

I **Sorry, we don't know either.**
II **One at a time, of course.**

Gremlins

Particularly well known to all aircrew in World War 2, these creatures have actually been around since the dawn of the flying age. They seem to have grown in number, with each stage in the development of flying machines. They multiplied prodigiously with the advent of the retractable undercarriage and again when jet engines with their cheaper fuel were introduced. Consensus has it that Gremlins are dwarf-like in build, although the current obsession with politically-correct language means that they should be referred to either as vertically-challenged, or persons of restricted growth (PORG).

They are notorious troublemakers and inhabit every corner of the aviation world – making life difficult for fliers. In this respect, it is often suggested that they receive much of their funding and some of their nasty habits from the CAA. Their evil ways include tampering with controls, so that they don't do what they are supposed to do (viz a recent Airbus A320 that would only turn right, causing some alarm to the pilots who wanted to turn left for Spain, but ended up in Moscow; suddenly moving the ground from beneath an aircraft, to make it stall and crash, and drilling holes in the sky ahead of an aircraft so it plunges several thousand feet in a matter of seconds, thus causing chaos in the cabin since this invariably happens when the meal is being served.

Gremlins have been known to use more devious tactics to cause trouble. These can include contamination of fuel and hydraulic fluid; tampering with braking parachutes so that they do not function properly; knocking bits off aircraft and helicopters in flight at inconvenient moments and most frequently of all, putting undercarriage levers into the 'up' or 'down' position after the opposite has been selected by the pilot. Aviation enthusiasts should always be aware of the omni-present PORG – it could strike at any time; and do note that it has a partiality for opening camera backs, before a film has been rewound, and actually chewing at films when they are in the camera.

Pre-flight Gremlin search by MiG-29 pilot. PRM

Hang Gliders

These are devices that some odd race of people, who live on the tops of hills or mountains, strap to their backs prior to leaping off and floating down to see Auntie Ethel who lives in the valley below. They usually find that she is out when they get there, so they turn round and climb back up the hill or mountain, carrying the device on their backs. They are so exhausted when they get to the top that they have to go home and go to bed, until the next day when they repeat the process all over again. No sane aviation enthusiast does anything other than turn and run when he sees one of these hang gliders heading in his direction. Although it is unpowered it is still rather heavy if it lands on you, and it is sure to do that if the chap wearing the device spots you before you have time to run. Hang gliders – avoid them at all costs!

Harrier

The Harrier is popular with enthusiasts and airshow audiences the world over, but distinctly unpopular with Argentine pilots, captains of Spanish freighters, Saddam Hussein's army in northern Iraq and the 'Keep Britain Quiet Brigade'. Like most successful British inventions, it has been successfully copied and exploited by the Americans. Why has McDonnell Douglas produced more Harriers than British Aerospace? Why have our European Union and NATO allies, Spain and Italy, bought their Harriers from America – and even called them by a different name (Matadors – Spanish Navy) to try to conceal it from us! Where do you think the next generation of Super-Harriers will emanate from?

Helicopters

Enthusiasts have very mixed feelings about these rotary wing devices. Like HM The Queen, they only choose to fly in them when they are unable to get to their desired destination by any other means. This usually involves flying over water to such as

'Otto, I said get a few litres of milk for the crewroom – not a darned cowful.' PRM

an aircraft carrier (and then only if the helicopter has flotation gear – they sink like a stone without floats) or to some remote hillside far from proper roads. REAL enthusiasts know that helicopters are basically unstable, like the pilots that fly them. One of this ilk stated that flying a helicopter was like driving up the M1 motorway and trying to draw a circle with your left hand and a square with your right hand, whilst still trying to weave your way through the traffic at 70mph. Why does a helicopter pilot sit on the right hand side of the cockpit and not the left, like pilots of normal aircraft ? A helicopter engineer described his company's helicopter in these terms: 'ten tonnes being lifted into the air by five flapping and rotating wings, that are held to the drive shaft by eight 10 BA bolts. If any one of those bolts, or indeed anything securing the main or tail rotors was to break, then the helicopter would fall out of the sky.'

The other problem with helicopters is that they are difficult to photograph properly. There is much controversy in the aviation press as to whether you must always include the whole of the main and tail rotor blades in your photograph, or chop them off to get a better balanced picture. We know that this has been done with an offending Spitfire propeller (the photographer was snapped preparing his subject by a rival 'keep propellers in the photo' advocate recently), but there is no documentary evidence that this has actually been done by a 'rotor blades out' aficionado. One word of warning, it is a dangerous practice to inspect helicopter rotor blades at close quarters when the engine is running, even though the blades might be drooping innocently in your direction.

Should one photograph all of the rotors?

Heroes

Most fields of human endeavour have their fair share of outstanding individuals and aviation is certainly no exception in this regard. Names like Amelia Earhart, Douglas Bader, 'Chuck' Yeager, Hanna Reitsch and Charles Lindbergh are writ large in the history of flying, by virtue of their exploits in pushing back the barriers, breaking records and combat.

The lives and careers of all those individuals are extremely well documented and need no repetition. Instead, here are some of my favourite heroes whose exploits are less well known, but who are just as deserving of a place in the saga of flight.

Sidney 'Wrong-Way' Throgmorton: A noted British philanthropist and fish restaurant owner, who endeavoured to become the first man to fly the Atlantic Ocean backwards. He did this by having the seat installed facing the tail of his Vimy, but became confused soon after taking-off from Floyd Bennett Field, New York and was last seen near Hoboken heading in a north-westerly direction.

Kleftiko Taramasalata: A Greek pilot who followed the traditions set by Icarus when he decided to experiment with man-powered flight. Early efforts were far from successful, and it wasn't until he began using a track-mounted trolley as a launch device that he first got airborne. All might have ended happily had he not struck the Acropolis a glancing blow which rendered him unconscious. Now completely out of control, his flight (and life) came to an end when he plunged into Piraeus harbour at terminal velocity. Today, a small plaque on pier 47 marks the spot where his remains were brought ashore.

The annual Freddie 'Biggles' Wade party is held at Old Warden.
BRIAN STRICKLAND

Freddie 'Biggles' Wade: Despite reports to the contrary, Freddie Wade was the inspiration for the celebrated books by W. E. Johns. Born and bred in Bedford, he actually learned to fly at Old Warden but his first solo sortie came to an abrupt end when engine failure caused him to force-land in a pond on the Shuttleworth Estate. Undeterred by this setback, he returned to Old Warden after a brief spell in hospital and again tried to make a successful solo flight, only to again encounter a problem which resulted in a second forced-landing in the same pond, this

time with more serious consequences. Badly concussed, he then stole an aeroplane and deliberately crashed into the pond, for ever after earning himself the soubriquet 'Biggles' Wade. Freddie never flew again, but did go on to have a distinguished military career with the submarine service. His dogged persistence was seized upon by Captain Johns whose novels and novellas inspired subsequent generations of children to consider flying as a career. The nearby town, previously known as New Warden, was re-named Biggleswade in memory of its famous son.

Historic Aeroplanes

There have been arguments about what constitutes a historic aeroplane for just about as long as the history of aviation and nobody is any nearer to establishing a method of classification, that is both accurate and acceptable to all. In the absence of a logical and coherent system, those who are interested tend to group them in four categories – although they are quite unable to agree just what each category means. After much detailed study, the following is offered as a guideline:

Antique Aeroplanes – Basically anything that can be found in the pages of an auction catalogue. Can theoretically include anything from a Sopwith Camel to a B-52.

Classic Aeroplanes – An aircraft of any type, the sighting of which encourages any type of aviation enthusiast to become very excited and begin emitting loud grunting sounds and other strange noises. Can theoretically include anything from a Sopwith Camel to a B-52, by way of Spitfires, Hurricanes, Meteors and even Hunters.

Veteran Aeroplanes – An aircraft of a type that is no longer in service. Can theoretically include anything from a Sopwith Camel to a B-52F (but not a B-52H).

Vintage Aeroplanes – An aircraft of a type that may still be in service, but not necessarily so. Can theoretically include anything from a Sopwith Camel to a B-52.

Latest arrival for the Jet Heritage Museum at Bournemouth is this Tornado GR1, as No 617 Squadron brings its Lancaster back on strength. PRM

IAT

The International Air Tattoo, usually held at RAF Fairford in July, is firmly established as the world's top military airshow. No other event attracts participation from so many countries, by so many different types of aircraft and brings aviation enthusiasts together for such a long period of time (if they can afford it). There are many other superlatives that can be levelled at this mighty event, which is organised in aid of the RAF Benevolent Fund.

As the IAT Directors Paul Bowen and Tim Prince have been running these Air Tattoos for nigh on 25 years, we have been instructed to devote a disproportionately large amount of space in this book to tell aviation enthusiasts just how wonderful the organisation is (a fact that you undoubtedly know already) and to expose some key members. The lid has been lifted just a touch by courtesy of one of its management team, ex Army Colonel Hugh Lohan. Yes, that's the first thing already pointed out – they come from all walks of life (Pongos and Crabs included), but they all have one thing in common – they share a total disdain for aircraft, unless they are parked quietly on the airfield, well barriered, with plugs in all the right places and the aircrew that brought them are at least 50 miles away in Bristol or London. They consider airshows to be OK until more than a couple of hundred people arrive, that's when they retreat into their bunkers to plot how they are going to snare up the departing traffic, without letting on to the police. You will recall that in 1993 they arranged a little incident involving a couple of MiGs. This gave the all-powerful Show Operations Centre (SOC – otherwise known as 'sock it to em') the perfect excuse to shut the airfield gates, until everyone had been searched to make sure that they weren't leaving with any video pictures of the accident that they might sell to ITN or Sky News. On that occasion the last people leaving the airfield, after the Saturday show, met the first arrivals coming in for Sunday's display. It was considered a triumph.

'Keeping all the balls in the air when you are running an airshow is a real headache', Tim Prince (centre) and Paul Bowen (right), directors of IAT. PRM

Another key group is the Sky High International Team who's pre-occupation is with loos. They task a group of scouts to tour the 15 loos, generously provided at great cost, to remove all toilet rolls, in case anyone has brought a small playful dog onto the airfield. They also move the loos from place to place, so that the needy don't have too walk too far to find one. They close any toilets that look as though they are getting over-used which, of course would present a hygiene problem, until the Sky High International Team can radio to Gloucester for the sludge gulper to be sent to empty it.

Well that's the top management, what about the rest of the cast of 20,000 shackled volunteers (that sometimes outnumber the paying public at IAT)? These are the unpaid, unsung and unfortunate heroes (and heroines) of IAT. But they have one thing in common with their superior directors, co-ordinators, managers, supervisors, foremen (and women) – they can't tell a

The volunteer who dared to ask the 'Show Operations Centre' (SOC) to sort out a problem.

Nightingale from a Blackbird or a Robin from a Falcon, at 50 paces. This is what separates the REAL aviation enthusiast from the IATs, although you might find one or two lurking somewhere in the middle.

We introduce you now to some of the worker bees whose unselfish efforts enable IAT to take place.

Emergency Services: A fine body of men with instant reaction to any emergency, no questions asked. Proof? – ask the Wren who got her suspender stuck on the catch of a third floor window at IAT 93.

Medical Services: Be it a heart transplant, a splinter, a headache or three choruses of Cwm Rhondda, they are always ready to oblige. There's no better place to be ill than at IAT!

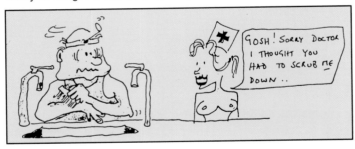

Aircrew Reception: Grab visiting aircrew before they have time to settle, load them with gifts, promises and booze, just to get stickers before anyone else has the chance.

'Now where shall I stick it?'

Communications: Have more crystals than a fortune teller's family gathering, and can perform miracles with the tin cans and smooth string. (It doesn't work with the hairy type.)

Commentators: Have been known to refuse to come down from their tower, unless the Teddy Bears' Picnic is played whilst they have tea.

Photographers: About 250 frustrated David Baileys. Previously briefed by Kodak that for every film they shoot, a 50p donation will be made to the retired IAT Volunteers 'Visit-the-SBAC-Show' fund.

Arena Manager: Manages to get grown men in vests and shorts chasing dogs through hoops of fire, and military bands to compete with F-16s. Incredibly, also persuades Air Marshals, Generals, Admirals and Mayors, to watch this activity in stony silence for hours without food or water.

Air Traffic Control: Tell the men in the aeroplanes where to go, when to come back, where to hold, (not the boy soprano), when to take-off and when to land. Generally a bossy lot and best left (like the commentators) in their own ivory tower.

Flight Operations: Tell the men in the aeroplanes where they are likely to go, when they are likely to come back, where not to hold (very much the boy soprano), and make sure they understand all the rules the tower will test them with. Usually much more tame than Air Traffic Controllers.

Information: Make sure that members of the public know where they are, who they are, and what they are. Sometimes look after lost children, when they have a lucrative arrangement with the caterers for those not claimed at the end of the day.

It's good PR to help the Kiwis back to their aircraft. BRIAN J ATKINSON

Flying Control Committee A bunch of killjoys who make sure the days of barnstorming are truly over. In 1989, stopped a Dutch F-104 pilot from flying through a Galaxy, just in case the Galaxy crew had not emptied the ashtrays, and the resulting cloud activated CND.

Press Centre A lot of busybodies who spend nine months before the show getting magazines and newspapers to print stories about it – and three months giving V-signs to those newspapers who asked for press passes, but didn't print any of the pre-show stories. Sometimes nearly as bad tempered as Air Traffic Control. The secretive and sinister BB is known to spend some time here.

Flying Display Organiser A post originally held by a Colonel Sanders after a Manager misread one of his FRYING TONIGHT adverts, and thought he was in touch with the Confederate Air Force. Now a very difficult job, as it involves getting eight hours of high flying turkeys into Matthews free airspace. It's a bootiful task.

The flying display organiser checks out each display pilot. PRM

Site Services Following their success in building a bridge to help Alec Guinness escape from the Japanese – will, at the drop of a TA weekend, build any type of structure over any obstacle, real or imagined. Can be identified by their Action Man outfits and whistling of Colonel Bogey.

Programme & Souvenir Sales By recruiting the local Mafia, this team ensures that one in every four visitors buys a programme. Forces souvenirs on to visitors who do not have the right purchase price in small change for a programme.

Icarus

Legend has it that a Greek named Daedalus was behind the first successful attempts to fly. This was an activity that he investigated in his spare time, when he wasn't otherwise engaged in building the Cretan Labyrinth. The system he chose to employ was based on the use of wings made of feathers taken from birds. These wings were secured to the arms with the aid of wax and flight was evidently achieved by flapping the arms vigorously. It must have been very tiring indeed.

All went well until Daedalus and his son, whose name was Icarus, set out to fly from Crete to the Greek mainland. If contemporary accounts of this journey are to be believed, at some point in the flight, Icarus became over-excited and ventured too close to the sun. In the process, he also became over-heated, which caused the wax to melt and resulted in him plummeting to a painful death.

What became of Daedalus is less clear, but there seems to be a possibility that, in the heat of the moment, he misread his compass and ended up steering a reciprocal course that eventually brought him to a landing point on the south coast of England, just a few miles from Portsmouth. Thousands of years later, his epic flight was commemorated by giving the Royal Naval Air Station at Lee-on-Solent the name HMS *Daedalus*.

Surprisingly, nobody has yet endeavoured to emulate Daedalus and Icarus by employing modern technological advances in the field of adhesive agents. It would be an appropriate way to mark the closure of the RN airfield in 1996, by a return flight to Greece. Perhaps John Travolta could be persuaded to re-enact the part in Greece Too.

Japanese

Not all Kamikaze pilots were Japanese – this Englishman tried it at Biggin Hill. PRM

The Japanese are looked upon with some measure of appreciation by the aviation enthusiast for their past great talents – inventing and producing the first recyclable aircraft and disposable pilots; some charming fighting machines with equally quaint names and catching the Americans with their trousers down at Pearl Harbour (or for US readers making a sneaky attack on the US fleet while it was resting at Pearl Harbor). After military defeat, the Japanese nation decided to take the Americans on at their own commercial game and proceeded to lead the victors a merry dance, in designing and producing high quality electrical and electronic goods, in particular. Enthusiasts around the world benefitted from this as they purchased and used Canon, Pentax, Nikon and Minolta cameras and lenses. They also produced their own top class aviation photographers to use this equipment, and in turn magazines with colour reproduction that turned the US publishers green (or yellow) with envy. And they're all still doing this today.

They wouldn't have smiles on their faces if this photo had been taken 50 years ago. BRIAN STRICKLAND

I don't think the Japs got it quite right when they copied this one! BRIAN STRICKLAND

Jargon

No other activity seems to foster as much in the way of abbreviations, acronyms, jargon and mnemonics as aviation, which is quite definitely plagued by terminology, that appears intended more to obfuscate than clarify. Even the experts are unable to keep track of all the examples that are, or have been, in use but here is a further batch to be learnt after you have scored 100% in a test on the list under 'designations'. These are all terms that a REAL aviation enthusiast can expect to encounter in the normal course of conversation with a fellow compatriot,

AWACS – Airborne Warning And Control System.
BOAC – Bought On American Credit or Boeing Only Aircraft Club.
CCIP – Continuously Computed Impact Point.
ECMO – Electronic Counter-Measures Officer.
GLCM – Ground Launched Cruise Missile.
OFO – Orbiting Frog Otolith
POT HEAD – NATO name for Soviet fire control radar
RAP – Rocket Assisted Projectile.
SAM – Surface-to-Air Missile (and not SAM Missile, as national daily newspapers will persist in saying).
SPONGE CAKE – NATO name for Soviet radar system.
TOW – Tube-launched, Optically-tracked, Wire-guided.
WSO – Weapons Systems Officer (also known as 'Wizzo').
   Yet more to follow later.

Jets

Jets are planes that do not have that cooling fan thing going round at the front, or on pods on the wings. They suck in air, and anything that gets in front of them, into their insides where they churn it all up, set fire to it, and spit it out at the back. There is a fatal fascination for both the front and rear end of jet-powered aircraft among all members of the public, when they attend air shows. They will first find an aircraft that is easily reached and then, after looking all round to make sure that at least a hundred REAL enthusiasts are trying to take

been mentioned and it is conceivable that they may be related to Mr Blobby. There is also speculation that Peter March is a distant cousin of Superman. Evidence to support this belief is that he seems to have the strange ability to be in several places at once and also shows a distressing affinity for telephone boxes. So far, though, nobody has tried waving Kryptonite at him to see what effect it has. The other theory is perhaps more feasible and is referred to as the 'Mad Scientist Theory', although that is perhaps a bit rough on genuine mad scientists – and mad scientists are people too, you know. This suggests that Peter has a secret laboratory somewhere (the Cheddar Gorge has been mentioned) where he spends his time busily cloning himself, with the objective of churning out lots of perfect reproductions. He seems to be succeeding!" (Hence, "Beware the tides of March"!

Do bear in mind that the question of how each of these two types got into the business of aviation journalism is actually irrelevant – the important thing to remember is that they are there keeping the enthusiast well informed or so they like to think. You should also note that genuine aviation journalists seldom, if ever, allow photographs of themselves to appear in print. They consider hiding their lights under a bushel (Sue or Bill will do) the key to their real success.

Journalists always enjoy enthusiasts haranguing them about the many errors in their ramblings. PRM

photographs, will stuff their heads up the tailpipes or intakes of the engines. Fortunately most of them do know when the engines are running, but there is going to be a memorable day when one of them overlooks this necessary precaution, and ends up very warm and spread across the airfield. This will be extremely messy, but it will solve all future problems of this type and enable the REAL enthusiast to take pictures without heads or legs doing a vanishing act in holes, where they shouldn't be.

Journalists

These are a different breed from the previously mentioned air correspondents. Aviation journalists in the main know their subject and write about it *ad nauseam* and usually to excess. There are actually two different types of aviation journalist. Those who stumbled into the business more or less by accident as a sort of extension of a childhood pastime (the Archers, Fosters and Peacocks of this world) and have never grown up. Those who didn't – a fairly small group that might appear normal and in full possession of their mental faculties, but do not allow yourself to be lulled into a false sense of security. They may not be completely barking mad, but anyone who willingly takes up aviation journalism expecting to make a reasonable living from it has to be slightly cuckoo.

"This is the larger category, but no one knows where it originates from", says Lindsay Peacock in the latest perorations on his pet theme. "There are two theories. The first subscribes to the belief that the March tribe may be an alien life form. In this context, the planet Blob (in the galaxy of Andromeda) has

Joy of Flying

This forthcoming new aviation magazine for the REAL aviation enthusiast, from the publisher of the best selling Joy of Faxing and Joy of Potholing magazines, will be on everyone's 'must buy' list, as soon as it is available. We were privileged to have a sneak preview of the first edition, the contents list (as follows) was quite stimulating. There are very practical and well illustrated features on: Safe Flying, Flying with Strangers, Flying Alone, Prone Flying, Flying for Fun, Flying Lessons, Flying for a Living, Flying for Learners, Flying for Lesbians, Flying Experiences, For the Love of Flying, Flying for OAPs, Unusual Flying Machines, Flying in Dirty Weather and Flying Dates for the Whole Year. There is an extensive classified ads section running to nearly 30 pages – it reads just like a telephone directory. Our eye was taken by this cryptic ad: 'Adventurous, but grounded young lady (30–ish) seeks young man with an aeroplane. Please send photo and details of aeroplane.' She's certainly got the making of a REAL enthusiast.

The readers' letters pages have some revealing correspondence, probably more fitting to an aviation agony aunt column. Here's just one of them: "Dear Joy of Flying, I am 16 and feel ready to fly. Is this normal? My Dad says he didn't have the urge to fly at my age, and I should wait until I've left college. My girlfriend says she would like to get off the ground with me as soon as possible. What should I do?"

Joy always gets as much pleasure from flying as she puts into it.

Junk

This might accurately be described as the aviation world's equivalent of all those unwanted household objects that lie around taking up useful space for a while, before being picked up and stuffed away in some corner of the loft, where they can conveniently be forgotten about until the time comes to move house.

Aviation junk falls into three different categories:
- *Wreckage* – Junk that remains after a crash or accident. Is often badly burnt and scarcely recognisable as having any intrinsic value. Some enthusiasts will pay huge sums of money for wreckage junk that dates back to World War 2.

Bit late on the touch down, but yet another bargain in the waiting for our Welsh scrappie who is currently re-equipping the South African Air Force. ROBBY ROBINSON

- *Scrap* – Junk that is left when a particular type of aircraft is retired from service. Scrap metal dealers are always on the look-out for this material and have been known to hang around outside RAF stations. They may attempt to bribe pilots to look the other way for a few minutes. They have been doing a roaring trade in Phantoms, Buccaneers and Canberras lately. The enterprising Welsh scrappie, who bought the fleet of Blue Circle Tornado F2s at St Athan in 1992 for just £100 each and promptly forgot about them, has just received a cheque for £15 million, and a free holiday in Rome, from the MoD who has bought them back from him, to replace the centre-sections of F3s damaged by careless workmen. They will be loaned to the Italian Air Force in 'as new condition'- the BC F2s had only flown 50 hours each around the Coningsby circuit, before they were rested.
- *Memorabilia* – Expensive junk, usually dating back to World War 1, when men were men and aircraft were basically off-cuts of plywood held together by glue and a few bits of wire.

Just worthless junk? Not really – it might look like scrap metal but underneath it's a vintage aircraft waiting for someone to spend the next 15 years (re) building. Then it will be worth something.

Kites

'Sling a sleeping bag under a kite and you've got a hang glider I suppose!' PRM

This was a popular descriptor for aeroplanes many years ago. You will be familiar with the term as a feature of RAF slang in World War 2 films. 'I took my kite out of the hangar and proceeded to beat the hell out of the Hun'. But you will not hear anyone referring to aeroplanes as 'kites' today. It is now used in its correct sense, to describe that paper or plastic device that is linked to you on the ground by a length of string, that you (or your off-spring) fly on a beach or a windy hillside. They are made bigger and stronger than ever before, and some are big enough to carry people aloft. There are serious kite fliers who hold regular competitions to see who can fly the most complex, colourful and highly manoeuvrable formations of kites, for a fixed duration without becoming entangled around you, themselves or the nearby trees. Kites should not be flown near to power lines, airports or in gale force winds, unless you want to go to join your maker. REAL aviation enthusiasts will know that it is illegal to paint any advertisement on a kite, if you intend to fly it anywhere within sight of the CAA, or one of its informants. You can paint what you like on a free or captive balloon of any size, but you mustn't advertise your favourite airshow, trendy clothing or make of camera on a kite!

Landing

This is the most important part of every flight, as you will well know by the applause from relieved passengers as the pilot of your holiday charter flight to Malaga persuades the Airbus A300 to remain on the runway after the third bounce and second approach in pouring rain and a raging crosswind. While a novice pilot will be allowed to take off on his third flying lesson, only the bravest (and most foolhardy) instructor will let him land the Cessna 152 before he has successfully graduated through his tenth lesson, and only then in ideal weather conditions.

The take off of most aircraft is simply a matter of power overcoming gravity. It simply flies itself off the ground with the pilot having very little input. On the other hand aeroplanes have a studied reluctance to return to make a landing while they still have fuel in their tanks to keep the engine powering them aloft. They will fight the pilot all the way down to the ground, and even then will play tricks on the pilot, particularly if they are 'taildragger' aircraft (that is, with a small wheel under the tail), that sits up and begs not to land. Most pilots will agree that a realistic alternative name for most landings is a controlled crash. A good landing is, *ipso facto* , one from which the crew and passengers walk away without any damage to themselves, the aircraft or the runway. It is quite surprising that this happens so frequently these days.

'You'll never get it on the lorry if you persist in flying in the opposite direction to the way it's going.' PRM

Every landing is a 'controlled?' crash. It's a good one if you walk away from it. ANDREW MARCH

While the principle of landing an aircraft is broadly constant across all aeroplanes, except Harriers, the techniques employed differ considerably from landing a very large aircraft like the Antonov An-225 and that for a tiny aircraft such as a microlight, but they are all controlled crashes. So why not give your pilot a silent round of applause when he gets you down on to mother earth safely after your next flight. The REAL aviation enthusiast would never make such a gesture to the pilot in public, of course. But just you watch all those fellow passengers' hands twitching in their pockets when you come to a halt a few feet from the end of Madeira's runway on your next holiday flight. (Don't look too closely, the twitching could have other causes).

'Have you ever had the feeling that something's about to fall out of the sky – with you in it?' PRM

Not as clever as this American chap who lands upside down – so he can keep watching the ground.' BRIAN STRICKLAND

Low Flying

'You asked for an arrival flypast.' DICK WARD

'Don't know why he's decided to land in the car park.' GRAHAM FINCH

This has nothing to do with personal remarks about zips, but has everything to do with training our front-line strike/attack pilots and our good friends in the EU and NATO – Germany. Since the end of World War 2 the RAF has had many squadrons of its aircraft permanently based in Germany. They have also done most of their operational training over the North German Plain and elsewhere over this huge country. Unlike the British, the Germans consistently put the government's image and its responsiveness to public demand ahead of the national and international defence requirements. One thing the German people claim not to like is fast jets flying low over their homes. Not their town houses, but their country homes that they mainly visit at weekends. As a result the Luftwaffe sends its pilots to learn to fly in the USA and its Tornado pilots and navigators then come to RAF Cottesmore for their next stage of training. All very nicely kept out of German airspace.

They bring down the wall, thus gaining the considerable expanse of the former East Germany to fly over, and the German government decides to severely restrict the RAF's low flying training. The British government's answer to this was to throw its toys out of the pram, disbanding as many of its squadrons in RAF Germany as it could, and letting the rest have reduced training in the low flying areas of Wales and Scotland in particular. So that is why you are much more likely to be attacked by a Harrier at 250ft and 350kt while walking in the Lake District, or paddling your canoe down the Wye Valley. Of course the REAL aviation enthusiast relishes the opportunity to see these low flying aircraft in their natural habitats, rather than penned up in a zoo-like IAT static park. Perhaps they should be forming a Plane Protection Society to enable the wild Jaguar, Hawk or free flying Tucano to roam the countryside of the British Isles at will. Maybe the League Against Cruel Sports will join them in their defence against the efforts of the wealthy farmers and landowners to hunt them from the skies.

If you camp near to an airfield, even a civil one, you can expect to have to keep your head down. PRM

Man-powered Flight

Before we get thousands of ladies, without bras, writing in to complain (OK we don't mind if you send a photo with your letter), this is the conventional title for 'person powered flight', and we've got too many entries under P. In any case, console yourself that in aviation history there is no recorded example of a lady intentionally launching herself into self-powered flight – only countless examples of nutty men.

Not that there haven't been many inducements for both men and women to try to get themselves off the ground and sustain forward flight over a measured distance. The famous Mr Kremer has been followed by John Major – remember the Flights of Fancy he kept advocating, Robert Maxwell, Richard Branson and most recently none other than the Secretary of State for Defence. His announcement that the MoD could no longer afford to buy fuel for the RAF's aircraft, since the Chancellor of the Exchequer had imposed a £5 per litre surcharge to pay the pilot's salaries, and redundancy payments to the last remaining 50,000 RAF personnel, came as a bit of a shock. In a written Parliamentary reply he said "A civilian contracting company (Airwreck Unlimited) at RAF St Athan has fortuitously come up with a modification to the Tornado's wings that means that they now flap rather than sweep. If the pilots can get themselves fit enough to move the handle fast enough backwards and forwards, then the Tornado will be able to sustain flight as fast and to a height every bit as good as the present versions. Airwreck, which is saving this government millions of pounds, has perfected a system to turn out wing-flapping Tornados faster than it takes a pilot to programme its computers. We have asked them to come up with a man-powered modification for the Harrier fleet. It would not be giving away too many secrets to the Americans if I tell you that it is likely to involve the swivelling nozzles".

Memorabilia

Be warned, most items labelled as original aren't, they're duplicates, replicas or copies. The trouble is that too many people watch that antiques roadshow programme on TV and think that if they gather up pieces of dusty junk, that they bought at last Sunday's car boot sale and send it along to an 'auction of aviation memorabilia', some gormless aviation person (not an enthusiast, of course) will buy it for a ridiculously large sum of money. Of course they do. The purchaser then parades his 'original fabric from Bader's crashed Hurricane' along with the Concorde first flight page from Brian Trubshaw's log-book in the Little Hampnet Museum. Before you know it, all the other villagers have come up with their memorabilia and you have enough material to fill the IWM at Duxford. The problem is that you have a pile six foot high of original Hurricane wing fabric and ten volumes of Brian Trubshaw's logbook.

'Go away, you're not parking on my front lawn.' PRM

'I don't consider I'm taking this military aircraft serial collecting too seriously.' RICHARD COOPER

Naturally, the REAL aviation enthusiast goes about the business of souvenirs (no, he doesn't call it memorabilia) in a very different and practical way. And that is as much as we are allowed to reveal here. There are some further clues in the photograph.

Military Enthusiasts

Military aviation attracts a much bigger following of enthusiasts than any other branch of aviation alone. It is possibly that military aircraft come in so many shapes and sizes, across a much wider spectrum than civil aircraft. They also carry a bewildering array of different numbers, letters, codes, squadron markings and other confusing forms of identification. These can be referred to as tail numbers, buzz numbers, serials, codes, etc etc. Military enthusiasts, like their civvy counterparts, collect the aircraft numbers, copy them into notebooks, cross-reference them, memorise them, categorise them and quote them at every opportunity. Do not be surprised to learn that whole books listing them have been published, and if you can imagine page after page after page of lists of numbers, then you are on the track of a bestseller. This aspect of the hobby is probably as close as it is possible to get to the age-old hobby of train spotting.

At air displays they will be seen noting every aircraft on the ground, in the air and hidden in hangars. Some will use a tape recorder and walk down the lines mumbling into it such phrases as "ZE783, Tornado F3, No 5 Squadron Coningsby seen Fairford 14 July 1993, two-tone grey, tail code CD in white, intake rim silver polished..." and so on. This will all be logged in a book, or these days on a micro-computer, and appear in a letter to *Aviation News* in ten years' time, when someone misquotes a Tornado F3 of No 11 Squadron, with the same serial and a different code. Never, never, question the authenticity of these people unless you have at least two hours to spare for each question.

One final word of warning, don't think you can become a REAL military aviation enthusiast by getting a crash course with the RAF. The Services are the last places where you can expect to find an expert on anything, let alone the markings carried by their aircraft. In fact, in March each year they are the first in the queue at W.H.Smith to buy the latest edition of Ian Allan's annual *abc of Military Aircraft Markings* – to find out where all their aircraft are, how many have been sold while on maintenance and how few are left to provide the nation's air defence.

Des Res – ideal for the couple looking for their first little Shack.
BOB ARCHER

'Let's get out of here, I think the war's begun'. PETER COOPER

Models and Modellers

Models have their value particularly when you want to get a Vulcan into the Palace of Westminster. JOHN CARPENTER

No this isn't the subject you thought it was from a quick glance at the title of this page. The photo above came in response to the compiler's request for an 'aviation model', so we've used it to accompany this bit of text.

Aircraft modelling is older than aviation itself, and some will argue quite strongly that those who pursue this very enjoyable hobby prove the point. The hobby can be divided into many categories, the two most interesting of which are probably Flying Models and Static Models. At some time in their life most of the former do, of course, fit into the latter description, these obviously being when they are being constructed and when they are not flying. The most popular of this type is the radio-controlled model. These can be made to scale when they represent miniatures of actual aeroplanes, or semi-scale when they look something like an original, or non-scale, when they usually look like nothing on earth. To the casual observer, the object of this part of the hobby appears to be to spend as much money as possible in fitting multi-channel radio equipment to enable the model to be controlled in the air, and as powerful an engine as possible – sometimes on very big models this can be from a lawn mower (an obvious, but crafty ploy because if the motor is at 2,000ft the lawn cannot be cut). The whole assembly, costing several hundreds of pounds, is then sent aloft and can come back to terra firma in a most spectacular fashion, making very expensive crunching noises on impact. This usually brings a wry grin (or grimace) from the owner, and cheers all round from spectators.

As interesting as flying models are, it is usually the non-flying scale model that attracts the overall aviation enthusiast, because in this there is a method of turning into three dimensions all the notes, sketches and evidence from photographs and drawings, that he has managed to accumulate at all the displays and museums visited during the summer months. What better way to spend a winter evening than whittling wood, or pulverising plastic, until it looks like the latest version of the Tornado, or the airliner that took the family to Benidorm.

'You come an inch closer and I'll have it off!' RICHARD ANDREWS

'I know which one I'd rather fly.' PRM

Museums

Aeronautical museums may be found in almost every country of the World and county in England (plus a few in Scotland and Wales for good measure). The quality of the items on display, and the facilities in which they are housed, vary to quite an alarming degree. There are those of course that are prestigious national collections – the RAF Museum at Hendon, the Imperial War Museum at Duxford, the Fleet Air Arm Museum at Yeovilton and the Museum of Army Flying at Middle Wallop (notice how the Army always have to put things ass backwards – it goes back an awfully long way to the time when they went to war on horses, rather than in helicopters). We digress. The remainder of the aeronautical museums and collections in the UK are mostly run by enthusiasts. This, of course, is largely an irrelevance when it comes to preserving aeronautical heritage, since the enthusiasts involved invariably spend 90 per cent of the time arguing about the accuracy of the colour schemes applied to the artifacts on display – and thus have little time or energy left to ensure that those artifacts are maintained in pristine condition.

'Call it a museum? Look's like someone's turned it over in the night.' DON CONWAY

As a result, what began as just plain junk usually ends up looking like shabby junk, although one or two collections have taken the process a stage further and now own really tatty junk. Admission fees do, however, usually take into account the degree of junkiness.

The rot sets in slowly. Most model makers start with a kit of an aeroplane that appeals to them, are quite happy to assemble it with care and paint it carefully. Then they decide to buy a book or magazine devoted to this part of the hobby and, in reading this, find that the model they have just made is an eighth of an inch too short. The most popular scale is 1:72, which is six feet to the inch, so it is immediately obvious how vital this error is.

This leads to a need to check other documents, which might reveal that the shape of the wings is wrong, the tail has too much slope on the leading edge, the cockpit is not rounded enough at the back, the undercarriage is too short – and so on. Instead of taking an objective look and thinking, 'It does look like the real thing in miniature and Aunty Mary will admire it, and only someone with a micrometer, reference to original drawings – and a total obsession with a level of accuracy that is never likely to be reached, will notice', the modelmaker throws it away and starts again. He is now on the slippery slope that leads to parts being used from ten different kits (much to the delight of the manufacturers) to produce one model. He will also become paranoiac with markings, correct colour tints, correct accessories and a hundred and one other minor details that really do not matter. This leads to a great increase in the quest for more information, which will see more time being spent reading, and listing questions to ask at next season's airshows. These are truly fanatical beings, who belong to a quite distinct branch of the species. Talk to any model-maker and the chances are that he'll be able to come up with all sorts of reasons, and explanations, as to why he enjoys his pastime. He might say he relishes the challenge of reproducing a particular type of aircraft in miniature. He might remark that he finds it relaxing after a hard day killing things at the abattoir. He might observe that it is satisfying, and rewarding, to witness the transformation involved in turning a set of parts into a complete object. But in all these he's really telling you that he is hooked, and doesn't know how to escape its clutches. The day is going to come when there is no more room in his house for both her upstairs, them that is at school, himself and his models. I leave you to guess which gets the chop.

'Mum, why's this tour of Bath taking so long? I didn't know the Romans had model planes.' BRIAN STRICKLAND

NATO Names

This Sukhoi Su-7UTI is Moujik *to the ears of the REAL enthusiast.*
PRM

Although the Russians today refer to the Sukhoi Su-27 as the Flanker and the Tupolev Tu-22M as the Backfire, neither the manufacturers, nor the Russian forces, gave them those names, nor the titles of every other military and civil aircraft flying in the USSR during the Cold War – they were all dubbed by NATO's Air Standards Coordinating Committee. The NATO ASCC, staffed by hundreds of highly paid, and very senior, military personnel, selected a name for every piece of military hardware, whether it flew or not, according to a set pattern – B for bombers, F for fighters, H for helicopters, M for miscellaneous – all highly original stuff. It went on through missiles, radar systems and electronic counter measures, but in a much more intricate and devious way. How they arrived at Big Nose for one such system is not readily apparent.

Whereas the 'names' were either printed in italics or between inverted commas until recently, because they were only reporting names for use by the military, when the countries of the former USSR and the aircraft manufacturers confirmed that they were calling the aircraft by these names themselves, they have become the official titles. Funny how things work out.

Of course the REAL aviation enthusiast has called these Russian aircraft by their NATO names for ever. But some of the names given to one-off prototypes are more obscure. Here's a selection that would puzzle most enthusiasts and send them scurrying for their reference books.

Barge	Tu-85 derivative of the Bull = Tu-4 copy of US B-29.
Boot	Tu-91
Brassard	Yak-28 = Brewer
Cart	Tu-70 variant of Bull (above)
Cash	An-28 derivative of Clod = An-14
Cookpot	Tu-124 derivative of Tu-104 = Camel derivative of Tu-16 Badger
Cork	Yak-16
Firebar	Yak-28P
Freehand	Yak-36
Harke	Mi-10 derivative of Hook = Mi-6
Horse	Yak-24
Mallow	Be-10
Mote	Beriev MBR2
Mystic	Mya M-17

Navigators

Although beginning with the letter N, navigators are a bit of an enigma for the unwary enthusiast. You might think it fairly self-explanatory – pilots drive and navigators tell them where to go.

Pilot snares a couple of navs, to return them from whence they came, if they can remember the way. BRIAN STRICKLAND

'Why does the Nav always drop his pencil down here?' PRM

'Funny, I could have sworn she said her grocers' shop was on this corner.' PRM

The trouble is, pilots don't like being told where to go by a failed pilot sitting behind them. Now if the navigator was sitting at the front, or alongside the pilot (as they did in the good old days), they would be much more use as they could see where they were going and simply point out the features to the pilot (who could also see where they were going). Pilots will tell you, with great relish, how much they are looking forward to the next generation of front-line aircraft, like the Eurofighter, where they will rule supreme, without any 'ballast in the back'. The navigator will retort with the comment that you can't rely on computers and, as pilots haven't learnt to read maps, they won't find their way back home, even if it is gin clear. But beware! It is unwise for any enthusiast to assume support for either side, since any member of an aircrew, pilot, navigator, flight engineer, male, female or not sure, will immediately join forces with a colleague to fend off an interloper.

Nicknames

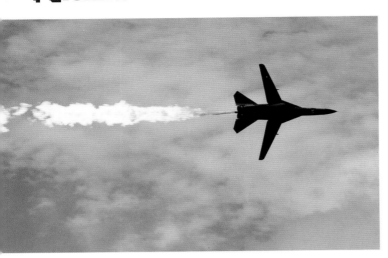

Australian 'Swingers' have been renamed 'The Hots'. GRAHAM FINCH

Often applied by the individuals who fly and service a particular type of aircraft, many nicknames are terms of affection and endearment, although some are undoubtedly meant to be far from flattering. The following listing is by no means comprehensive, but does include examples that have found widespread acceptance among pilots, technicians and enthusiasts alike. The REAL aviation enthusiast knows all these names (and many more besides – some that are unprintable or the publisher has censored) and ALWAYS using them in conversation.

Aardvark – General Dynamics F-111
Albert – Lockheed C-130 Hercules
Aluminium Overcast – Convair B-36 or Avro Vulcan
Chippie – de Havilland Canada DHC-1 Chipmunk
Dragon Lady – Lockheed U-2

Double Ugly – McDonnell Douglas F-4 Phantom II
Fat Albert – Lockheed C-5 Galaxy
Flick Knife – Panavia Tornado F.3
Flying Coffin – Lockheed F-104 Starfighter
Goat – Grumman HU-16 Albatross
Herky-bird – Lockheed C-130 Hercules
Hog – Republic F-84F Thunderstreak
Hookey-Tookey – Kaman SH-2 Seasprite
Huey – Bell UH-1 Iroquois
Hummer – Grumman E-2 Hawkeye
Hun – North American F-100 Super Sabre
Jug – Republic P-47 Thunderbolt
Meatbox – Gloster Meteor
Rhino – McDonnell Douglas F-4 Phantom II
Rook – Sukhoi Su-25 'Frogfoot' (translation from Russian 'Grach')
Sled – North American F-100 Super Sabre
Slidy Top – British Aerospace Harrier (GR3 only)
Sluf – Vought A-7 Corsair II
Stoof – Grumman S-2 Tracker
Stringbag – Fairey Swordfish
Swinger – General Dynamics F-111
Tee-bird – Lockheed T-33
Thud – Republic F-105 Thunderchief
Turkey – Grumman F-14 Tomcat
Wart Hog – Fairchild-Republic A-10 Thunderbolt II
Whistling Wheelbarrow – HS Argosy
Whispering Death – Bristol Beaufighter
Whispering Giant – Bristol Britannia
Widow Maker – Lockheed F-104 Starfighter
Wobbly Goblin – Lockheed F-117A Nighthawk

Finally it should be added that it's not just aircraft that get nicknames. The US Navy's aircraft carriers also have their pet names, so if you hear mention of the *Big John* they're talking about the *USS John F Kennedy* or the *Ike* then it's the *USS Dwight D. Eisenhower*, and so on.

'The Group Captain said to use the cheapest means – so I called the AA, 'cos I'm a member.' PRM

Operation *Granby*

This is the rather grand title that 'those who spend their time devising such things' gave to the RAF's activities during the Gulf War. Everyone else called it Desert Storm. Perhaps this is more fitting as the 'storm' blew itself out before it could wreak ultimate havoc on Saddam Hussein. REAL aviation enthusiasts all have their favourite images of the unique nose art that adorned RAF and USAF aircraft operating in the Gulf, and are hoping that it will reappear when the inevitable sequel, Desert Storm II, takes place.

RAF Tornado F3 crews, here on a recent exercise, are getting prepared for next year's Desert Storm Part Deux. Nige Marks

Ornithopter

Man (and possibly woman) has always wanted to fly like the birds. The distinctive feature of a bird's flight is that its feathered wings flap rhythmically. But this has been the stumbling block in the production of a replica bird (or ornithopter). You only have to watch the opening sequence of *Those Magnificent Men in their Flying Machines*, or go to the end of Eastbourne Pier when foolhardy individuals try jumping off to impress their 'birds', to see some of the disasters that result from avian mimicry. Man has designed helicopters, supersonic jets, spaceships and gliders, but has still failed to replicate bird flight.

Various attempts have been made, and some top secret experiments have been, and are still being, carried out. Readers of the first edition of this book will recall the report of a squadron of Hunters that were camouflaged with feathers and persisted in heading south despite every effort by the pilots to stop them. During the Falklands War some swift thinking by the RAF led to feathers being stuck over the wings of another squadron of Hunters and they departed for the South Atlantic. Fortunately they managed to reach Chile in record time without air-to-air refuelling and were immediately put to good use. The authenticity of this report has been verified by enthusiasts who noted the sudden disappearance of a number of Hunters from RAF Brawdy, and their mysterious reappearance on the strength of the Chilean AF. The RAF denied all knowledge of these aircraft, claiming that they had never existed.

Reports from REAL aviation enthusiasts in the USA indicate that strange bird-like aircraft have been flying at night over northern Nevada. It is well known that birds have a low radar print (ask any Tornado GR1 pilot) and they are very stealthy. Lockheed has successfully managed to replicate this in its latest product from the Skunk Works. Unfortunately, flight trials are proving very difficult, as large numbers of birds always join up in formation behind it and cause considerable congestion. The trail of mess on the ground is leaving a track that is identifying the location of the secret aircraft and its base.

He doesn't look like a bird, can't flap his arms fast enough, hasn't got any feathers and doesn't sing sweetly – the only thing he has in common is the size of his brain.

'You'll have to flap those wings a bit harder than that, son!' PRM

'OK clever clogs, who's going to sort out this mess?' PRM

The first visit of the Lockheed Superbird to the UK ended in disaster. While flying high over southern England one night last September it collided with a mysterious circular object that had taken off from a cornfield in Wiltshire. After crash landing at Boscombe Down it was discovered that the crew had been killed despite having extra thick shells to protect them. It is believed that the failure of this project has resulted in the veteran Blackbird being brought back into service.

Parachutists

These are aviation nuts who choose to leave a perfectly serviceable aeroplane, at a ridiculous height above the ground, because a green light comes on and someone says 'jump'. There's worse to come. Once out of the plane they soon realise their stupidity and try to fly to safety. They spread their arms and legs and think they can glide down to mother earth. Looking around as they plunge earthwards they see the other former passengers doing the same thing and the sky is very crowded. Several of these wackos have smoke billowing from their trouser legs – they think they're the *Red Arrows* – poor souls. When it's almost too late they use a ring to pull out a bit of nylon string

'They do a good impression of the Red Arrows' *Diamond Nine. But wait 'til you see their formation landing – it's a real cracker!'*

that opens a bag they are carrying on their backs, in the hope that a nylon sheet falls out and catches the air. This assumes that they have remembered to put it there in the first place, and have folded it the right way after stuffing it back in the bag to go home after the last time they jumped.

Now suspended below what resembles a duvet, if they are lucky they are drifting down towards a nice soft piece of ground, well clear of their fellow parachutists – or at least that is how a normal person would want it. But no! The parachutists have one thing set in their tiny minds – they all want to land on the same point (either in the middle of a cross on the ground or a large firework that is belching out white smoke). To achieve this they hold on to one another, stand on their shoulders or even their duvets. It's quite alarming. When it is all over and the last parachutist has hobbled over to the target that he has wisely missed by a wide margin, the pilot of the empty, but perfectly functioning aircraft, flies past as if to underline their madness. While many of these parachutists (we are sorry to say) are men, there is the occasional female who responds to this lemming call. No REAL aviation enthusiast will ever be seen partaking or showing any interest whatsoever in this irresponsible activity. Now, the aircraft that has cast out these poor unfortunates is a very different matter.

'Hope they've seen that F-16 aiming for the same spot!!' PRM

Passengers

'Get your flaming elbow off my head, it's bad enough giving up my seat to this chap Shackleton.' PRM

Airlines are using new techniques to persuade their 'victims' to board the aircraft. BRIAN STRICKLAND

These are the people who pay for the dubious privilege of flying in an aeroplane, usually an airliner. There is disturbing evidence of a trend by some airlines to try to dignify the process of being crammed into a long tube with hordes of other sufferers, ordered about by a bunch of officious individuals in uniform, strapped to uncomfortable seats for hours and forced to eat a very poor representation of food. These long-suffering unfortunates are now being referred to as customers, clients or, even worse, as guests. By employing terminology of this kind, the airlines hope to make flying appear more user-friendly. What a pity they are wasting their effort on trying to dress up what is almost always an exhausting (and sometimes harrowing) experience by playing silly games with words. They should settle for describing their passengers as victims. Then we'd all know where we stand.

Of course amongst the large number of 'victims' that fly about the world there are those masochists who say they actually enjoy it. The exception always proves the rule. There's the chap who has flown backwards and forwards across the Atlantic on Concorde more times than many of us have had roast dinners. Unfortunately he got so much ahead of himself through all this supersonic flying that he ended up getting on to Concorde one day at London and New York at the same time, and hasn't been seen since. It's believed he de-materialised in mid-Atlantic.

'You vill come on board my aircraft right now.' BOB ARCHER

Turning the pages of the Guinness Book of Records you will discover the story of a former REAL aviation enthusiast who has sadly given up his pastime and succumbed to the lure of flying as a passenger. No, not like the lady who has flown over 8,000 times in a Loganair Islander, this appropriately–named Edwin Shackleton flies only once in any particular type of aircraft before giving it up in disgust to seek another type that he hopes he will like better for his return journey. Amazingly, to date he has flown in 540 DIFFERENT types of aircraft! He says he intends to keep on flying in new types until he finds one that he really likes.

ₚhotographers

Well you can see them at any airshow, airport, microlight fair or balloon meet, the 'keep Kodak smiling' brigade of aviation enthusiasts with their multiplicity of cameras, lenses, gadgets and bags. No wonder they call the films 'Gold', they must be the next nearest thing to owning a gold mine for the manufacturer. If you look at aviation photographers as a breed you will quickly discover that they fall into four categories: the novice, the casual, the serious and the dedicated photographer. How do you recognise each of these genres?

The 'novice' aviation photographer (otherwise known as the NAP) invariably possesses an enormous metal camera case that is literally covered with stickers, most of which commemorate past air displays that the owner may, or (more likely) may not, have attended. This camera case is an extremely heavy object and hence the need for it to be trundled around on wheels and left as a trap for unsuspecting people to fall over. It is akin to a black hole, in that it swallows anything around it – vacuum flasks, packs of sandwiches, odd shoes, seven different types of film, many filters and lens hoods but no camera! The novice has spent so much money buying the all important status symbol in the first place that he had little left for cameras. Consequently, the NAP actually takes photos using Aunt Bertha's little Instamatic, which he keeps in his anorak pocket.

The 'casual' aviation photographer (CAP) usually has a slightly smaller metal case that he uses to stand on as he is almost invariably too short to take photographs over the top of the barriers. His case is also covered with gaudy vinyl stickers commemorating air displays, most of which he has attended. The casual photographer often forgets to do up the hasps of his case before attempting to jerk it into position, and then spends several minutes retrieving empty film boxes, lenses, camera bodies, copies of *Amateur Photographer*, batteries, cleaning tissues and all sorts of other detritus that spilled out when the lid flew open. It becomes immediately apparent that he has the largest collection of those funny little brushes that blow air out when you squeeze them, and can reel off their countless uses. He is also incredibly learned about the merits of particular types of film, lenses and cameras, having spent inordinate amounts of airshow time boning up on their attributes courtesy of *Amateur Photographer*. The CAP will willingly discourse on these topics for hours at a time to anyone prepared to listen. Sadly, despite all this knowledge, he still has not mastered the art of taking a good photo of a moving aircraft. He is very much a still life photographer.

The 'serious' aviation photographer (SAP) invariably has a

'Boss, no-one wants to buy this film, they say their cameras aren't big enough to get it in.' BRIAN ATKINSON

canvas camera bag with lots of little pockets on the outside. These are normally filled with sandwiches, bananas, crisps, chocolate bars and other types of sustenance, for the serious

Meet the serious aviation photographer en route to an assignment. No room in his bag for cameras etc – it's filled with culinary delights. RICHARD COOPER

photographer is always hungry due to spending prodigious amounts of energy–sapping time waiting for the perfect moment to take a picture. His camera bag is not covered with stickers, mainly because they don't adhere well to canvas – and therefore keep falling off. The SAP carries a stepladder as a matter of routine (and as a counterbalance to his bag) and is incredibly adept at swinging this free from his shoulder and erecting it in a single smooth movement. The serious aviation photographer is utterly clueless when it comes to the technical aspects of cameras and photography, having learnt his craft from mistakes rather than from manuals. The SAP is adept at obtaining decent results in difficult circumstances and can swear fluently at members of the public who get in the way when he is about to press the shutter. He has had at least one picture published in an aviation comic and uses this to obtain press facilities for the next five years.

The truly dedicated aviation photographer (DAP) is very rare. There is currently only one breeding pair, and their nesting site is such a closely guarded secret your chances of encountering them are slim. However, they sometimes emerge around the time of IAT, so you might like to know how to recognise this rare species. The DAP employs several assistants – one to carry his bag; another to drive and erect the cherry-picker; a third to carry his film; a fourth to change film and pass him his cameras; a fifth to operate the funny little brush that blows air out when you squeeze it and a sixth who has the map to work out where to go next. Suffice to say that the dedicated aviation photographer considers himself to be the only true professional aviation photographer (PAP) and wouldn't be seen dead in the company of any of the aforementioned categories. Given this attitude, though, he just might be!

Pilots

'Hi Tracy – see you after the show.' PRM

'Falic 21 outbound to the Tailhook Convention.' PRM

A great deal has been written about pilots and the REAL aviation enthusiast probably knows quite enough to pick one out in a crowd at 50 paces. What has not been committed to print so far is one of their less appealing characteristics. So, from an American computer Bulletin Board service, this collection of some of the most common porky pies uttered by pilots.

'I'm 29, got 6,000 hours, a university degree and 4,000 hours on Belfasts and I'd love to fly with a woman pilot.' PAUL GINGELL

We will be on time, maybe early.

Excuse me, miss, I seem to have lost my Concorde keys.

All that turbulence spoiled my landing.

I'm a member of the Mile-High Club.

I only need glasses for reading.

I'm sure I've got the field in sight.

I became visual at Decision Height.

If we get a little lower, I think we'll see the lights.

The weather is OK, it's going to be VFR.

Don't worry about the extra on the loadsheet, it'll fly.

I have no problem flying across the Atlantic on two engines.

No problem – I've got thousands of hours in these aircraft.

No need to look that up. I've got it memorised.

Of course I know where we are.

I know that the gear was down.

The doc told me to cut my drinking by half, so I did. I cut out the mixer!

And a final word on pilots from 'Airline Magazine': The average pilot, despite the sometimes swaggering exterior, is very much capable of such feelings as love, affection, intimacy and caring. These feelings just don't happen to involve anyone else...

'If we get a little lower, I think we'll see the lights'.

Plane Names

One thing's for sure, there have been lots of strange aircraft built in the past 90 years or so and equally there have been many with weird names. The REAL aviation enthusiast will be able to give the answers (eventually) if confronted with any of these trivial questions about the names of aircraft. If you want to confirm your claim to being one of that elite band, you can check the solutions on page 52.

1. What was Airwolf?
2. Why was the Reid & Sigrist Desford renamed the Bobsleigh?

3. What was the name given to the enlarged, civil version of the Westland S-51 Dragonfly?
4. What was the Short Seamew?
5. Did the ill-fated de Havilland DH 108 research aircraft have a name?
6. What two manufacturers have had Valiants in service with the RAF since 1960?
7. What different names were given to the USAF's and US Navy's DC-9-30?
8. Which of the following nicknames have been given to the F–4 Phantom – *Double Ugly, Elephant, Rhino, Tomb, Hammer* and *Old Smokey*?
9. Who was, or is, the *Dragon Lady*?
10. Which RAF aircraft were individually named after the characters from a children's TV series?

Preservation Groups

Discover something aviation-related that is old or interesting, and a group or collection will be set up to preserve or renovate it. Most aviation groups will give an infinite number of reasons why someone – usually the mythical 'they who accept the blame for everything' – should have had the foresight to preserve:

● Every film replica aircraft ever built
● A sample of every bomber or fighter that saw action in either World War
● Flying examples of every Hunter used by the Swiss Air Force
● The entire Czechoslovak Air Force (before it was divided)
● All Sunderland flying boats
● Surviving East German Air Force Mi-24 Hinds
● Guy Gibson's dog
● The remains of von Richthofen's Fokker Triplane
● The Wright brothers' shoe laces
● The pen Harold Wilson used to cancel the TSR2 contract
● The TSR2 jigs
● Every mark of Shackleton or Canberra
● Two Phantom and three Lightning cockpits

This list is endless and, reading through the columns of their many and various publications, you will find that there is much more to come. There are countless tales of crates of complete Lancasters, Hampdens, Defiants, or whatever happens to be in vogue at the time, found buried in a quarry in Norwich or under tons of scrap in breakers' yards at Longbridge. If any of these really exist it is hard to say, but the REAL enthusiast looks upon them with some scepticism until someone produces a list of the serials of these relics and photographic proof.

Membership can be very rewarding but, like modelmaking, it is too easy to become obsessed, and the convert can soon find himself involved in compiling thousands of useless statistics such as how many shoe laces were lost in the Falklands, to the number of half-inch pop rivets in a Lancaster tailplane, to the serial of every type of aircraft that has crashed in the Himalayas on a Good Friday. All this forms a part of the rich tapestry of the world of the aviation enthusiast, and our intentions are to guide – not to recommend or condemn. (Special Offer! - Any Group recommending this book will be advised, under cover of a plain envelope, of the whereabouts of two brand new Bell P-39 Airacobras, still in their crates, concealed on 11 May 1942 in Russia.)

PLANE NAME ANSWERS

1. **A modified Bell 222 for the TV series of the same name.**
2. **It was given a long nose for prone pilot trials.**
3. **Westland Widgeon.**
4. **An anti-submarine single engined aircraft that went into production but saw very limited service.**
5. **Yes, unofficially the Swallow.**
6. **Vickers (Valiant) V-bomber and Schleicher (ASW-19) winch-launched glider.**
7. **USAF = C-9A Nightingale; USN = C-9B Skytrain II.**
8. **All of them.**
9. **Lockheed U-2.**

Publications

REAL enthusiast Bob doesn't try to hide what his favourite airshow reading is. PETER COOPER

Aviation magazines and journals, both so-called professionally produced and amateur publications, are a minefield for the unwary. It has to be very much a case of 'you pays your money and takes your chance'. Some are dominated by very strong personalities, with their own personal views and preferences that are reflected throughout; some have a 'holier-than-thou' attitude, which gets up the noses of REAL enthusiasts, while others try to be all things to all men (and women) and fail badly. A recent 'sign of the times' is the appearance of two female editors in what was previously a male domain. You can tell where they are heading by the use of the word International in the titles of their magazines.

Some publications concentrate on modern aviation, others on vintage air events and historic aircraft, some on the world-wide scene, and yet more on every possible facet including magazines for pilots. Very few manage to cover all they set out to with any great success, and if you select what appeals to you, and stick with it, you will eventually find that it will cover everything, for there is only one basic subject and eventually all that is written is regurgitated and will appear in most magazines over a period of time. Those just reporting Concorde's entry into service are obviously well out of touch and should be avoided.

You can pick out the smug, self-satisfied, flypapers by their wild (and often unjustified) claims that they are the 'most widely read', 'biggest selling', 'best illustrated', 'most accurate', etc, etc. You can also tell from the cover price, the number of colour photographs, accuracy of editorial, quality of paper and its 'feel' whether a magazine is 'value for money'

There is also a wide range of so-called enthusiast publications which are often no more than sheets of duplicated paper, run-off on a second-hand duplicator with leaky rollers, and photographs that look like Belisha's original drawings for his pedestrian crossing.

The only advice is to do what most other people do, that is to visit the local multi-national newsagents and read all the aviation magazines. This should be done by placing your chosen reading material between the covers of *Mayfair, Penthouse, Fiesta* or *Forum*, otherwise people watching you will think you are some kind of pervert.

Pubs

Some enthusiasts collect aircraft serials or registrations, or take photographs, while others just enjoy watching planes fly. But there is also a more select and esoteric group – you can pick them out by their garbled speech and uncertain balance – that 'collect' aviation related hostelries. As you would expect, most public houses with aviation related names can be found near to airfields, so this thirst quenching hobby can be shared with the normal pursuit of real aeroplanes rather than real ale.

Latest in aerial pubs. There's even a handy first-aid kit should you fall down the steps on the way to your aircraft. BRIAN STRICKLAND

'I heard that pilots are a thirsty lot, so I decided to set up my bar where trade would be brisk.' PRM

'It's no good trying to disguise yourself – the leather jacket with pens is a dead give-away.' BRIAN STRICKLAND

Where do the aviation pubologists find their quarries? Well there's The Comet Hotel near to the late lamented Hatfield and the Britannia and Wayfarer pubs near to Filton. The Harrier is close to RAF Wittering, as the Swordfish is to Lee-on-Solent. Famous pilots like Sir Douglas Bader, Baron von Richthofen (The Red Baron) and Samuel Cody are all immortalised in the names of public houses.

So you can quickly build up a long list, if you have the perseverance and the thirst for this unusual collection. There are airport names, inventors, aerobatic teams, aircraft components and even UFOs all on signs waving in the wind to entice you in. It takes a lot of bottle to admit that you are only visiting a pub to add it to your 'list' without sampling the best brew it has available. You have to be quick, though, to catch the latest development – the flying pub. Converted military aircraft are now attending some airshows with literally 'everything on tap'. Ground crews are getting used to setting up the 'facilities' on the flight lines to keep their aircrew happy before and after their displays.

Quotations

Aviation and associated activities are a rich source of highly quotable material, a few examples of which are presented here. Note that some of these quotes may be apocryphal, and one or two may also be out of context. To avoid legal complications most of them have been left 'anon'.

'If I slide down here it's going to ruin my evening.' PAUL GINGELL

- *I can see no practical military use for the aeroplane.* Orville Wright.
- *When in doubt, mumble. When in trouble, delegate.* RAF Staff College.
- *If it jams force it. If it breaks it needed replacing anyway.* A/C 2 Plonk.
- *If you don't think you're the best pilot in the business, MAYBE you're in the wrong business. If you think you could never make a mistake, you are REALLY in the wrong business!*
- *Don't ever let an aeroplane take you someplace your brain hasn't gotten to two minutes earlier!*
- *Remember, an aeroplane flies because of a principle discovered by Bernoulli, not Marconi.*
- *Man will never set foot on the moon.* – Sir Harold Spencer Jones (Astronomer Royal), 1957.
- *PanAm hired gentlemen with the expectation of training them to become pilots, Eastern hired pilots hoping to train them to*

'I say old chap, do you mind moving over a bit, it's difficult to see the runway.' PRM

become gentlemen. Neither carrier was successful in its efforts.

- Wheel landings are a crutch for the incompetent!
- The reason they give airlines names is so you can tell them apart, they're all alike really!
- Bugger Bognor! Unidentified Red Arrow.
- What! You say the Feds are accusing me of doing a barrel-roll around that Convair 580 with my T-33? Uh —-, do you think they'd buy total electrical failure, spatial disorientation and loss of all radios?
- Son, you're going to have to make up your mind about this wanting to be a pilot when you grow up, you can't do both!
- It is a bluff my dear Ernst. They can make cars and refrigerators but not aircraft. Hermann Göering, 1941 (speaking to Milch about America's aircraft production).
- Arguing with a pilot is like wrestling with a pig in the mud, after a while you begin to think the pig likes it. General Dynamics.
- If you're faced with a forced landing, fly the thing as far into the crash as possible. Bob Hoover.
- People want to have an airport they can get to in five minutes in order to board an airliner that won't make any noise over anybody's house.
- Young man, was that a landing or were we shot down? Little old lady in row 3-C.
- A helicopter is a collection of rotating parts going round and round and reciprocating parts going up and down – all of them trying to become random in motion.

- If the pilot survives the accident, you'll never find out what REALLY happened!
- You know, the Japanese really don't like us, as a matter of fact if they had better wine and could cook they could be French! Pilot of a Northwest Airlines' Boeing 747, number 13 in the hold to land at Tokyo.

'The Gladiator – 10 to one at Newbury.' ATC

Rattling the Bars

This is the aviation enthusiasts' equivalent of going to a zoo and irritating caged animals by dragging a stick along the bars of the pen or, of the slightly more childish activity, of ringing someone's door bell and then running away and hiding before they answer it. Sorry to say most enthusiasts do it to some degree, although the technique and persistence varies according to the nature of the interest.

This enthusiast is definitely having his bars rattled. BRIAN STRICKLAND

Civil enthusiasts really have only one significant way in which they can 'rattle the bars'. In its simplest form, this involves a gaggle of enthusiasts occupying every table in the cafeteria at any airport, thus preventing passengers from being able to find a seat. More advanced forms of the activity include visiting the cafeteria counter with a polite request for a glass of water, credence being added to this request by the production of a bottle of pills, which must be shaken loudly in front of the manager. (Note: the pill bottle doesn't really need to contain any pills – Smarties will do just as well and have the added advantage of producing a very convincing rattling sound).

Military enthusiasts have a very different activity, which is usually aimed at irritating airfield security forces. This is done by acting suspiciously and repeatedly approaching the perimeter fence, only to disappear whenever anybody from inside the base investigates. The best results are obtained when this exercise is repeated several times in quick succession. Stepladders are a particularly useful adjunct, since they can give the appearance of a break-in attempt if observed from a distance. Marginally more subtle is the concept of crashing about in the undergrowth that often surrounds airfields. If done well, this can produce really spectacular outbursts on the part of security forces, especially if they have previously been called out to investigate suspicious behaviour at different locations on a number of occasions.

Records

A considerable amount of energy used to be devoted to setting new marks for aircraft flying the fastest, highest, longest and with the greatest amount of concrete – but not all at the same time. In the 1950s hardly a day went by without someone, somewhere, breaking some record for something or other, mainly for the simple reason that aviation was still progressing in leaps and bounds. Usually, such exploits were undertaken by Americans, but the Russians sometimes got in on the act and rumour has it that even the occasional Brit managed to go fast enough to claim the World Air Speed Record at least three or four times in the post-war era when the Americans weren't looking. Nowadays, not too much effort is devoted to breaking these records, but REAL aviation enthusiasts will want to know about a recent British attempt on the World Landing Speed Record (Class A: Variable Geometry Aircraft – Wings Swept). We therefore publish in full this agency report.

"While development work continues on his new 'Thrust II', record-breaking car, Richard Noble has not been idle. Not content with being the fastest motorist in the world today, Noble recently attempted to establish a new World Landing Speed Record for variable geometry aircraft, with wings fully swept.

Using a Tornado aircraft, taken out of storage specially for this record-breaking attempt [BARG confirms that it was ZE154 that had its wings accidentally welded in the fully swept position by a civilian contractor in 1990], Noble chose a top secret military airfield in the south of England as his operating base. However, on the day of his attempt Noble was established on final approach to the airfield when he detected an irritating knocking noise coming from somewhere behind him. Noble elected to overshoot, and abandoned his record attempt for that day. The knocking sound was later discovered to be the clattering of his navigator's Rosary Beads from the back seat of the aeroplane.

Sadly, before he was able to organise another attempt on the World Landing Speed Record, Noble was pipped to the post by the four-man crew of an American B-1B Lancer bomber which landed at its home base, wings fully swept, at an amazing 237 knots. Owing to the stressful nature of this particular record breaking mission, the B-1B crew had all been issued with brown flying overalls and, shortly after landing, were driven away from the aircraft at high speed to 'freshen up a bit', according to a US Air Force spokesperson.

On closer inspection of the aircraft, servicing personnel found that the B-1B was actually resting on its wheel hubs, and a team from tyre manufacturer BF Goodrich was then called in. They will try to establish what became of the tyres during the record-breaking landing run.

In the meantime, the local Sheriff's Office, close to the base, has detained a number of youths in connection with the tyre incident in case the Goodrich team is unable to establish sound scientific reasons for the disappearance of the B-1B tyres". Rioters News Agency, 1995

Red Arrows

'I said wear Red Arrows *strip for the briefing – not take your clothes off.'* PRM

'That'll teach you to wave to your girlfriend in the crowd when you're landing.' PRM

Originally named the *Yellowjacks*, presumably because they were all naval pilots of oriental origin, or maybe RAF pilots who had previously worked for the AA, the RAF's *Red Arrows* aerobatic team has just celebrated its 30th birthday. As REAL enthusiasts will know this bunch of pilots are the *prima donnas* of military aviation in the UK. Mind you, they have an awful lot to learn on that score from the *Thunderbirds* and *Blue Angels* in the USA before they can get the ultimate, world-wide, accolade.

The *Reds*, as they prefer to be called, wear red flying overalls (instead of green gro-bags like all normal RAF aircrew) so they can be instantly recognised wherever they go. Their hair is styled by Salvatore Dalia, make-up is by Yves Guzzi and body toning courtesy of the Fergie Salon in down-town Lincoln. They are immensely popular with the public, despite the team's relentless efforts to douse them with oily smoke at every opportunity.

'What's funny about this? We make birds fly wherever we go – day or night.' PRM

Like most show-biz stars they have their faithful followers and Red groupies who idolise their 'heroes of the air' and follow them to watch every performance. Mind you there are no other pilots, navigators or aviation enthusiasts amongst this number. It might be jealousy or perhaps it is simply that they don't like the RAF devoting itself entirely to the team from May to September.

No other fliers (except the Queen – and she has to share now that her flight has disappeared after Prince Charles made rather a mess of one of her 146s) have their personal jet aircraft cleaned, polished and prepared for every flight they make; their own reserved airspace; cars to meet them at their destinations; beds in the best hotels if they are away from base; an annual all

'I wish you'd make up your mind which way we're going.' PRM

'Quick put 'em away chaps, I think we've been spotted.' PRM

'He's always trying to get in on the act. Let's see what he thinks of a barrel roll.' PRM

'Now I always knew there was a right way to get into this darned cab.' PRM

'1, 2, 3, j..., 4, 5, ...um, 6, 7, 8, 9, 10, 11 – no I can't.' PRM

'Hand you over I vill to Squoodron Laser Big Red Ears how vill tell us about zee Dead Sparrows.' PRM

'Tell you guv, that's worth two of your plastic ones any day.' PRM

expenses paid holiday in Cyprus; regular free trips to the continent and most of August at the seaside. No wonder they cannot cope with the good life for longer than three years. Usually the leaders then go off to fly private VIP jets for the likes of Nigel Mansell, and the team members either join RAFAY Pacific or fly a Virgin plane.

But times they are a-changing. The *Red Arrows'* extravagant life style has fallen under the gaze of the hatchet men from the Treasury. By the end of the decade they will have to be self-financing. Strenuous efforts are being made to obtain commercial sponsorship. Before long you can expect to see the team in newly painted aircraft bearing the sponsors' logos,

cleaning, refuelling and servicing their own aircraft, bringing bicycles and camping gear with them to shows and charging for autographs and stickers after the display. Check the oil in your car before you set off home, though. They have been seen at a garage near Scampton learning how to drain sump oil from cars without opening their bonnets, then dashing back with overflowing cans to put it into their Hawks' smoke systems. And after the display season ends? They have been signed up by their sponsor to sell cleaning products around the country. Watch out, you might be closing your front door on a Red Arrow Better-Klean Round the Bend salesman next winter – so do find out first BEFORE you slam it.

'I know you're the Synchro leader, but you'd do much better if you had the map the right way up when you are on the ground.' PRM

Registrations

Owners often decorate their aircraft to match its registration. PRM

For the benefit of those enthusiasts reared only on a diet of military serials it is best to explain what these 'registrations' are that civil enthusiasts go nutty about. These are the identification markings applied to aircraft owned and operated by civilian organisations, companies, airlines and private individuals. Most commonly, these registrations use five or six letters with a dash after the first or second letter. Some countries, notably the USA and Russia have alpha-numeric combinations. Specific prefixes are allotted to individual countries. For example 'G-' is allocated to British registered aircraft; 'HB-' for Switzerland; 'N' for the United States of America; 'F-' for France, 'RA-' for Russia and '6V-' for Senegal.

Registrations usually have five characters such as G-BASS, HB-PUB, F-PINT and 6V-JAR, but may include as few as two (e.g. N1) or as many as seven (e.g. RA-76718). Further information may be had from publications like Ian Allan's *Civil Aircraft Markings* or from members of Air Britain.

Rules & Regulations

Aviation is hide-bound by rules and regulations. You cannot build, repair, modify, service, buy, sell, park or do absolutely anything involving an aircraft without it being regulated or ruled upon by such as the Civil Aviation Authority. Even a free-flying powered model aircraft or a kite is subject to regulations. Some of these are eminently reasonable on the grounds of safety, many are not. Although the rules change with great rapidity, as the CAA discovers another way to either make life difficult for the private individual and/or extract more money from him before letting him indulge in his aviation activity, there is a hard core of sensible 'flying regulations' that has been around for some 75 years. First published in 1920 these US Army Flying Regulations are still relevant today. Aviation enthusiasts are well advised to heed them and make sure that any pilot that they are foolish enough to take to the air with, pays proper attention to them.

1. Don't take the machine into the air unless you are satisfied it will fly.
2. Never leave the ground with the motor leaking.
3. Don't turn sharply when taxiing. Instead of turning sharp, have someone lift the tail around.
4. In taking off, look at the ground and the air.
5. Never get out of a machine with the motor running until the pilot relieving you can reach the engine controls.
6. Pilots should carry hankies in a handy position to wipe off goggles.
7. Riding on the steps, wings or tail of a machine is prohibited.
8. In case the engine fails on take-off, land straight ahead regardless of obstacles.
9. No machine must taxi faster than a man can walk.
10. Never run the motor so that blast blows other machines.
11. Learn to gauge altitude, especially on landing.
12. If you see another machine near you, get out of the way.
13. No two cadets should ever ride together in the same machine.
14. Do not trust altitude instruments.
15. Before you begin a landing glide, see that no machines are under you.
16. Hedge-hopping will not be tolerated.
17. No spins on back or tail slides will be indulged in as they unnecessarily strain the machines.
18. If flying against the wind and you wish to fly with the wind, don't make a sharp turn near the ground. You may crash.
19. Motors have been known to stop during a long glide. If the pilot wishes to use motor for landing, he should open the throttle.
20. Don't attempt to force the machine onto ground with more than flying speed. The result is bouncing and ricocheting.
21. Pilots will not wear spurs while flying.
22. You must not take off or land closer than 50 feet to the hangar.
23. Never take a machine into the air until you are familiar with its controls and instruments.
24. If an emergency occurs while flying, land as soon as possible.

Riding on the steps, wings or tail of a machine is prohibited – especially if you are the pilot. PRM

Serials

These are the identification markings applied to aircraft of military ownership and operation. As the title implies, these usually take the form of numerals, but some air arms use alpha-numeric combinations while just a few use a serial system that uses only letters. The US armed forces have a system that only uses numerals (e.g. 158999 that is carried to identify a Navy F-14A Tomcat and 64-18240 that is on an Air Force C-130E Hercules). In Britain, an alpha-numeric system is used with examples being XZ450 (a Fleet Air Arm Sea Harrier FA2) and ZE706 (an RAF Tristar). All-letter serial numbers (yes, it's a contradiction in terms!) are much less common, but Cameroun's Air Force is an example, with a CM.170 Magister bearing TJ-XAX.

Bear in mind that regardless of which system is employed, these military identification markings are always referred to by serious enthusiasts as serial numbers and never as registrations (qv). This is because most serious enthusiasts have no real knowledge of what a contradiction in terms is – all they're interested in are the numbers...or the letters and numbers...or the letters and ticking them off in their dog-eared copy of Ian Allan's annual *abc of Military Aircraft Markings*.

Slang

Aviation slang is widely used in conversation by anyone who has even the most tenuous links with aircraft and flying. Slang mostly seems to originate with the military, but REAL aviation enthusiasts have also made their own rich contribution to this fascinating subject. Examples of this type of language, from both sources, are given in the list that follows. It is worth bearing in mind that the amount of slang used by a particular individual is often found to be in inverse proportion to the extent of his or her connection with the aeronautical world. So, unless you wish to convey the impression of being a nerd – or, worse still, a dweeb – I would recommend moderation when employing terminology of the following kind.

Bang seat	Ejection seat
Bins	Binoculars
Bomb-burst	A formation manoeuvre in which a group of aircraft dive towards the ground and split to head off in a number of different directions; or a tactic used by enthusiasts to lose an escort by simultaneously heading off in several directions
Bounce	To initiate a surprise pursuit of other aircraft, or catching a fellow enthusiast doing something he shouldn't
Box	Radio
Chopper	Any type of helicopter
Cloggie	A Dutch enthusiast
Cop	Aircraft serial or registration seen for the first time
Crab	RAF personnel

Plebs – *all of them.* PRM

This 'rock ape' is actually a 'driver'. We've always suspected a bit of monkey business goes on in the RAF. PRM

Driver	Pilot
Duff gen	Inaccurate information (there's a lot of this about)
Fish-heads	Royal Navy/Fleet Air Arm personnel
Gawper	Someone who stands looking at an aircraft, accident, etc for an undue amount of time
Gen	Information or a disparaging remark about a badly informed spotter
Good gen	Accurate information
Gopping	Unsatisfactory (usually re weather)
Grice	A 'super-cop' – a really rare aircraft/marking seen for the first time
Jostle	Enthusiast's encounter with police or any other form of authority
Loadie	Loadmaster
Log	List of serials or registrations of aircraft seen on a particular day at a specific place
Pleb	Any member of the general public who attends an air show
Pole	Telescope
Pongo	Army officer; in aviation terms an Army Air Corps pilot
Prod	Air-to-air refuelling with the hose and drogue method of transfer
Rock ape	Member of the RAF Regiment
Scrape	An aircraft that has been re-registered

SGT	Self-Guided Tour – used to describe wandering around inside an airport or base, without permission, or after losing the escort
Spiking	To employ a laser designator as a means of marking a target that is to be hit with laser-guided bombs. Originates from US 'Pave Spike' pod designation system
Superpole	Big and powerful telescope
Superspotter	An obsessive aviation enthusiast – sometimes also called a 'gricer'
Trash-hauler	Any military transport aircraft
Two-holer	Any two-seat combat aircraft
.... and so on, ad nauseam	

Societies

There are many 'professional societies' that are dedicated to the furtherance or study of aviation. These should not be confused with those that are 'up-market enthusiast groups' calling themselves societies to achieve a 'higher' standing. Like aviation groups they publish newsletters which vary in quality of print and content, but in the main are different because they try to introduce editorial comment which can be hobby horses of the president, chairman, treasurer, secretary, membership secretary or editor; in many cases these will all be the same person.

The aims and objectives of most of these fringe societies can be identified by their titles, many of which focus on a particular type of aircraft or are based on geographical locations. They all have one thing in common, the 'society' is known by its acronym rather than its title. Here's just a small selection.

AIDS – The Avro International Devotees Society meets at Woodford under the wing of Vulcan XM603 for its AGM on the last Saturday in June each year.

BBLBS – Bring Back Lulsgate Bottom Society was formed by a number of local residents who want to restore Bristol International Airport to its former glory as RAF Lulsgate Bottom. They meet in the former station commander's house at infrequent intervals.

AIDS at the Houses of Parliament. The Avro International Devotees Society about to meet under the wings of its Vulcan in London. JOHN CARPENTER

BABBS – *The Beccles and Bungay Beaufighter Society.* Formed to commemorate the part played by the ladies of the area in knitting socks for Beaufighter crews. Both members meet every third Tuesday in 'The Bull'.

CLOTS. *Crewe Lancaster Operations v Trains Society.* Dedicated to trips flown by Lancaster crews against European railway systems (not post-war). All six members, plus two dogs, meet in the waiting room of Crewe station (by permission of BR).

CRAPS – This *Colchester Rocket and Projectile Society* is somewhat esoteric, but it is said that its regular meetings go with a bang.

RAWLYS – *The Red Arrows-We Love You-Society* meets in the Scampton village hall at 10pm on the first Thursday of the month. Unfortunately, it has been given notice to quit the premises that are to be converted into a Job Centre.

It is essential that anyone who wants to be recognised as a REAL aviation enthusiast should belong to at least one of each type of society or it will be assumed that they are not taking their interest seriously. In the main these societies are quite harmless, and if you have a tie and jacket you can attend their meetings, but make sure that you don't fall into the trap of taking them as seriously as they take themselves!

potters

The origin of spotting goes back to the First World War when fighting aircraft were new on the battle scene. The gunners in the trenches found it very difficult to pick out the enemy's aircraft when they were flying overhead. The ever-cunning Huns had the idea of painting target spots on the undersides of the wings of Royal Flying Corps aircraft. Special infiltrators were trained to crawl into airfields at night and apply the spots. These 'spotters' did such a good job that the RFC mechanics thought the aircraft looked rather pretty and proceeded to paint red, white and blue concentric spots on all the aircraft. To avoid any confusion the Germans decided to paint a black cross on their aircraft, to tell the gunners not to shoot at their own aircraft.

During WW2 spotting took on a new meaning – still associated with recognising aircraft though. The Royal Observer Corps devised a system of flash cards showing the silhouettes of warplanes to train members of the Corps to identify aircraft as they flew overhead by spotting their main differences. Those who passed the test were awarded with a spotter's badge. With the disbanding of the ROC this meaning of the word spotter has fallen by the wayside.

Today the word spotter is associated with enthusiasts who keep lists or logs of aircraft they have seen and keep very detailed records of serial numbers and/or civil registrations (see earlier references). With the advent of portable computers, word processing packages, cd roms and all the other electronic paraphernalia of modern living, there is probably no aircraft, flight or aviation activity in the UK that does not get recorded for

RFC aircraft were given large aiming targets under their wings for the benefit of the German gunners. PRM

posterity. These spotters are also very pro-active and spend a great deal of time pointing out to editors and publishers of aviation magazines and books (if they dare to quote registrations or serials) just where they might be going wrong.

Stars

These are the celestial bodies that aircrew can use for navigation when all else fails. They are seldom used these days, since the taking of star shots requires the use of a device known as a sextant. Unfortunately, few navigators can remember how to operate one of these and most of them actually experience great difficulty in even finding where the box that contains the sextant is stowed on the aircraft. A further obstacle to successful celestial navigation is that the really important stars (like Sirius, Canopus, Naomi Campbell, Kevin Costner and Patrick Moore) can only be seen at night, which isn't a lot of use to anyone who gets lost during the day.

A further problem for the navigator, once he has mastered this celestial tool, is the need to have an up-to-date print out of the star guide, published every day on page three of the Sun. By the time that the navigator gets the allocated copy from the aircraft captain this page is invariably missing. Sadly, even with the aid of Russell Grant's weekly guide to the stars and motorway roadwork black-spots, hardly any navigators are able to read star signs properly. From general experience there aren't many navigators who can read road signs properly either, that's probably why Tornado GR1s keep flying backwards and forwards along main roads and motorways in Scotland and Wales, much to the pleasure of holidaying aviation enthusiasts.

Tornado GR1A at low-level down the A47 looking for roadsigns to point him the right way home to Marham. PRM

Stealth

'I will get that serial number if it kills me. Can't keep the pole still, knew I shouldn't have had that extra one last night in the bierkeller.'
RICHARD COOPER

Much has already been said about this subject, so perhaps we should not give anything more away that might assist a potential enemy. Suffice to say that the REAL aviation enthusiast has learnt a great deal about moving unseen and un-detected by radar on or near airfields.

'Comrade, that chap sunbathing there with all his clothes on says he's a prince. Very suspicious. I think he is taking photographs of our jet amphibian. Let's bring him in for questioning.'

The skills of stealthy aviation spotting (SAS) are being honed to perfection on courses at the new enthusiast's training centre near Hereford.

Stickers

Vast quantities of plastic stickers (mostly the circular variety) are circulated at major airshows around the world every year. They are produced by show organisers, participating air arms, squadrons, and even individual aircrew as well as commercial organisations. Some are advertising or promotional material, others representations of squadron crests and badges. Many are humorous and all are highly collectible. They are used as currency for bartering and can be a valuable means of 'opening locked (hangar) doors' when enthusiasts travel abroad. Stickers turn up in the most unlikely places, often very far from where they originated. They often seem to have a quite unexpected durability even when attached to an irregular surface.

Using stickers to 'zap' objects, people or even aircraft is a childish activity that the REAL aviation enthusiast is unlikely to indulge in. It is considered funny to zap an aircraft door on the inside with a sticker that reads 'toilet' on it, or 'MOT failed' on the rear end of a Tornado F3 after it has just landed. The IAT volunteer who stuck a large zap on the nose of a Russian Bear at Fairford, covering its unit marking, was last seen with a bunch of enthusiasts heading for Whipsnade Zoo with a jar of honey strapped to his head.

Well and truly zapped, but you can't call her stuck up really. BRIAN STRICKLAND

Living dangerously – these zappers are covering up this Bear's unit markings. BOB ARCHER

Sub-hunters

Rarely captured on film, the finale of one of the sub-hunters more unusual tactics is enacted as the aircraft descends through 1000ft. The drumming sound is thought to attract submarines to the surface. PRM

Yet another RAF sub-hunting ritual, whereby the wail of bagpipes drives people into the sea. If they see a submarine they report back to the man with a flag on his head. Much fuel is saved by this means. PRM

1942

1992

"An anti-submarine patrol is incredibly monotonous and there is great difficulty keeping alert and even awake. On one occasion the pilot flying the aeroplane fell asleep..." EXTRACT FROM REPORT BY RAE TEST PILOT FLT LT A F MARTINDALE, ATTACHED TO NO 120 SQN, MAY 1942. (CARTOON BY TIM NEWMAN)

Superspotters

Possessing a degree of fanaticism of an order of magnitude several times removed from that of your average civil and military aviation enthusiast, the 'superspotter' is only rarely seen, mainly because he seldom stays in one place long enough to be visible to the naked eye, although you might catch a glimpse of the shock wave if you are very fortunate. He will usually arrive in a huge cloud of dust, 'do a base' and depart instantly on the never-ending quest for more numbers to feed his voracious appetite. He thinks nothing of driving all the way to Ramstein, Germany to see two Israeli F-16 Fighting Falcons on delivery. He is utterly obsessed and ceaselessly driven – he is a man apart.

'Superspotters' are an entirely European phenomenon. There are several in the United Kingdom and at least one in Germany, but by far the greatest concentration is to be found in Holland. Or, at least, it would be, if they'd do us all a favour and stay there for intervals of more than ten minutes at a time.

The best known British one is reverently referred to by his colleagues as 'The Wraith', for the simple reason that, like ectoplasm, he has the ability to pass through solid objects. This is a talent that comes in useful for gaining access to securely locked hangars and other structures that contain aeroplanes.

The nearest equivalent to a group of Dutch 'superspotters' in the animal kingdom is a gaggle of geese. Both groups are gregarious by nature and can generally be found in packs (sometimes up to several hundred strong); both groups share a tendency to expand to fill every available space; and both groups are given to honking loudly and continuously.

There are several superspotters in the UK. PAUL GINGELL

Superspotters have a handy knack of persuading the No 4 bus from Boscombe to Bournemouth to divert via Fairford or Mildenhall. PRM

Superspotters Spotted

To help you identify the Superspotter (SS) when you meet one, these photographs will give you some essential clues.

In this photograph, the SS is at the top of the steps – he is studying the inside of the Tornado's cockpit while the 'plebs' are distracted by an aerobatic team. PRM

No, it's not the Peacock but the penguin that's the real SS. PETER COOPER

This 'gaggle of geese' (we know they're Dutch because of their bicycles) are starting to strip for action. You can almost hear the honking as the F-117s arrive. RICHARD COOPER

And I don't think these are SSs in the usual sense, although they do seem interested in peering into unusual places. BRIAN STRICKLAND

Only an SS would go into a burning aircraft to get its serial before it is reduced to ashes. PRM

This multi-legged TOW missile carrier is definitely not an SS. They don't collect missiles. RICHARD L WARD

Take-off

This is the process by which enthusiasts remove their outer garments in order to reach their essential 'tools of the trade', albeit their 'poles' for scoping distant targets; notebooks for getting down important details or more film for their cameras. It also has a more direct aviation meaning as it is used to describe the precarious state when an aircraft powers down the runway and fights against gravity to leave the ground. Just as soon as the state of flight has been achieved the pilot's attention shifts to getting that aircraft back down onto the ground and safely under the influence of gravity, for what is euphemistically called a landing. Pilots spend many hours and vast sums of money learning to manage these manoeuvres successfully.

These two young lady wing-walkers were grounded by the weather at a Cotswold airshow. Helen and Caroline – the exhibitionists that they are – decided to walk on the top of the fire truck while the pilots displayed for the crowd. PRM

What they didn't know was the evil plot that the Crunchie boys had lined up to expose these two young ladies.

OK it was a bit of a cheek, but it certainly amused the watchers.

The moral of this unlikely tale – if you want to keep your clothes on don't stand on top of a fire truck at an airshow or you will be classified as a REAL aviation exhibitionist.

Tankers

'Hey – you down there – you're supposed to suck not blow.' PRM

Tankers are the only aeroplanes that take-off with much more fuel than they will ever require. They then lay in wait to refuel other aircraft that took off without enough fuel to get where they wanted to go, or have decided to stay airborne for longer than they originally thought. Tanker crews are among the bravest (although others will argue that they are the silliest) fliers in the world. Tanker crews are usually in very strong positions to become prima donnas – but its best not to fall out with them, especially if you are in a receiving aircraft.

The RAF's tanker fleet of recycled former British Airways VC10 airliners is commended in the latest awards made by the Green Leaf Veggies party. The service is planning to enter its

'I think it's going to take quite a while to drain this bus.' ANDREW MARCH

Blue Circle Tornados, that are being brought back to life for the Military Air Fighters of the Italian Air Force (MAFIA), in next year's competition.

'Always in with a good idea these tanker boys. Fancy filling up the tanks with Coke and selling it for half price on the hottest day of the year'.

Then & Now

Aviators are very nostalgic people and often hanker for a return to what they misguidedly call 'the good old days'. What they don't realise is that in many instances those days are still very much with them, its just that they don't see it as the REAL aviation enthusiast does.

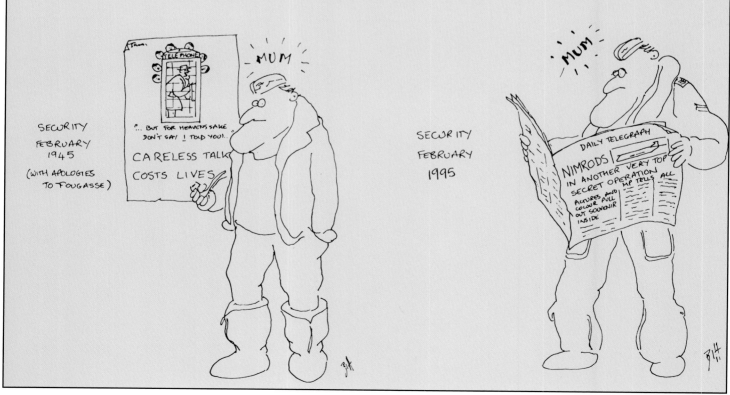

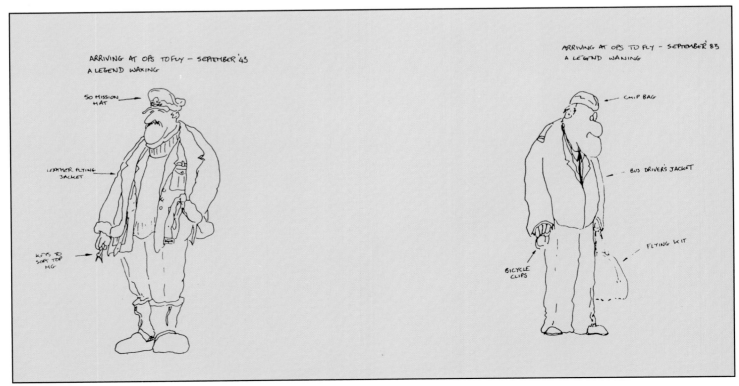

Tornado

When British Aerospace owned the Rover Group, transfer of aerospace technology to Rover resulted in cars that were both faster and more aerodynamically shaped. But have you ever wondered what benefits Rover brought to British Aerospace? Well ponder no more – for the answer is here! The new TORNADO CR1 (Cabriolet Reconnaissance Mk.1).

The aircraft is shown here on an early test flight from its top secret base somewhere in the north of England. MoD Programme Manager for this latest addition to the Tornado family is Air Vice-Marshal Bertrand (Bertie) Strapford-Cash. He had this to say about the project:- "This is the aircraft we've been waiting for. Under 'Options for Change' this is the healthy option. No more stuffy cockpits shrouded in perspex and no more nasty pressurisation systems cluttering up the works – from now on our chaps will be breathing good, old-fashioned fresh air. Without a doubt, this aircraft brings together in a single airframe the high-tech of today and the romance of yesteryear – supersonic speed and open cockpits. This aircraft will go a long way towards reminding the young chaps of today what air combat was like in the old days – wind in the wires, the sun in your face, the smell of castor oil – ah yes, those were the days.

Tractors

These somewhat ungainly machines are an everyday part of the airfield scene. Tractors are used to pull aircraft out of hangars, tow items of equipment, pull the grass-cutter and a thousand and one other things. Although not usually driven by farmers, when they are – like our friend Charlie Kulp – they are likely to cause problems.

Indeed, this aircraft is so retrospective, the crews will be able to smell the nostalgia going down the intakes!

"Not only that, – this aircraft saves us lots of lovely money too. Doing away with the canopy and all that gubbins will save the RAF a real packet but in addition, with this aircraft we can do away with all that expensive Infra-Red recce kit too. From now on, our chaps will be able to take their own cameras up with them and, if they see anything interesting while they're out on patrol, they can lean over the side and pop a few happy snaps for the Intelligence blokes back at base.

"We have had to make one concession to the crews though. We've left in the cockpit heaters because, in winter, it can get a bit nippy over northern Bosnia, and there's nothing worse than cold feet on a long mission".

The Tornado CR.1 is set to enter service late next year, when flight trials are completed. An export version, aimed at customers in the Gulf states, is also being considered, and will feature leather trim, sun visors and a racy 'go faster' stripe on the fuselage sides.

Charlie ploughs his fields, plants crops, harvests them and flies his plane to round up his wayward cows in exactly the same way – with gay abandon. ANDREW MARCH

Charlie Kulp, seen here flying his
Piper Cub, qualifies for the title of a
REAL aviator. ANDREW MARCH

It isn't widely known that in their quieter moments (usually when no-one is
looking) airfield based tractors have been known to do a spot of flying
themselves. This Case International Tractor was captured on camera very
early one morning by insomniac REAL aviation photographer Paul
Gingernell. So as not to attract the attention of the sleeping airfield staff,
the tractor shut its engine off until it was over the open countryside.

U-2

'I'm sure the undercarriage was here when it took off.' PRM

One of the most famous aircraft of the Cold War era, the Lockheed U-2 is the world's highest flying glider (or so we are led to believe). Based on a British-designed torch battery, when it really mattered the Power (sic) failed and it came down in Russia, much to everybody's surprise. Its flight plan, filed before it took off from RAF Moreton-in-Marsh, was supposed to be to Timbuctoo to count the grains of sand in a small area of desert, as a builder from Epping was reported to be illegally exporting it to Saudi Arabia.

This was one of the biggest navigational errors in the history of aviation, and led to much shouting from the Russians that the U-2 pilot, Gary Powers, did not have a Russian visa in his passport. The US government immediately denied that such a plane existed – and promptly re-designated all its U-2s at RAF Alconbury as TR-2s – the TR intended to fool the Russians into thinking that they were gliders for training the local Huntingdon Air Training Corps squadron. Funny that they called them U-2s again as soon as the Berlin Wall came down.

The other dubious achievement of the Lockheed U-2, as avid readers of the Guinness Book of Records will undoubtedly tell you, is that it holds the record for the highest number of landings without half of its undercarriage. In fact it has only managed to return to terra firma on seven occasions with all the wheels that it took of with. It is also quite fascinating that the U–2/TSR-2 has the highest number of landing collisions with fast moving Ford Mustangs.

One of the many occasions when a landing U-2/TR-2 has found a Ford Mustang competing for use of the runway.' PRM

Undercarriage

'I thought they guaranteed to get here within 30 minutes.' PRM

An undercarriage is the wheeled part of an aeroplane that is supposed to be lowered before landing. In order to keep airport fire services in training, pilots regularly pretend that they are about to land without the advantage of their wheels being in position to enable them to roll along the runway. Despite the flashing lights, horns, red-flares fired from the ground and the advice of air traffic controllers, some aircraft do actually attempt wheelless landings. This can be quite spectacular, but of course does save a lot of tyre wear.

On one occasion during the Second World War, a pilot was transferred to flying boats from heavy bombers. One day he decided to take his flying boat and visit his former colleagues. As he lined up to land at the airfield, the runway controller, seeing a huge flying boat about to cut a furrow down his runway, fired off a red Very light. This reminded the pilot he was not flying an aircraft with wheels... he returned to his base, lined up and carried out a perfect cross-wind landing on his hull and floats... then, all smiles, stepped out of the flying boat straight into the sea.

'Are you sure the undercarriage is down?' PRM

Variable Geometry

"This is actually one of the few bits of aviation-related terminology that I can claim some vague knowledge of", writes that well-known guru of the aviation enthusiasts Linseed T Pincock. "Mainly because geometry wasn't one of my better subjects at school and I'm not ashamed to admit that my answers always varied. To some extent, I guess I could claim to have pioneered variable geometry, although my teachers probably didn't see it in those terms. Part of the problem was to do with the fact that I was quite unable to even say 'isosceles' let alone visualise it. As for the square of the hypotenuse, all I have to say on that score is that I lost count of the number of hours I spent staring at those wretched drawings hunting for squares. It was a complete waste of time, because all I ever saw were triangles".

"As for algebra", he burbles on, "that was completely Greek to me and I never did manage to figure out the logic of letters that were supposed to relate to numbers. It quite spoilt my enjoyment of books for years afterwards, since I was never sure whether they were meant to be read – or solved. And if you've ever tried solving an Agatha Christie, you'll know exactly what I mean when I say it's difficult...".

There are of course several aeroplanes that employ the principles of variable geometry in their design, most notably the Panavia Tornado. The reason for the variable sweep of its wings is the typical international battle that is established practice – whereby no-one will ever compromise – the Germans wanted a 25deg sweep, the British a 35deg sweep and the Italians a 55deg sweepback with turned up wing-tips. The upshot, after five years of negotiating – everyone gets what they want (except the Italians of course) with variable sweep.

Veteran & Vintage

Some pedantic people will argue that flying and aviation have not existed long enough to have any established traditions... there are just habits. It is perhaps wise to adopt the terminology used in the 'old' car world so that we can at least include some definitions that have become regular parts of the aviation vocabulary, although it is very much a case of each to his own. Vintage is generally accepted to mean those built between the years 1917 and 1930. So corroded hulks of aluminium and fabric, usually with two sets of wings and enormous radial engines, that have been found on rubbish tips, in scrap yards or dug-up from reclaimed fenland, and are waiting to be rebuilt by

The Anglo-German-Italian Perfectly Anglicised Never Again Variable Instant Aeroplane-Tornado fighter. PRM

'I know about these new curly propellers – but I can't fathom why it should have a plastic container just attached to one blade.' PRM

enthusiast groups, are Vintage aeroplanes. But as with most things, the term has become abused and is often used to describe any aeroplane about which one or more people feel inclined to write to an enthusiast publication expressing horror that it (the subject matter) is about to be scrapped. This means that Canberras, Jet Provosts, Hunters, Buccaneers and VC10s (if not still required for conversion to tankers) can all become Vintage aeroplanes, proving the pen is mightier than the scrap hammer.

To overcome these shortcomings it is not uncommon to hear the term Classic Aeroplanes (in hushed whispers) used to describe both the V & V and those that don't fit either category.

Therefore a 'Classic Aeroplane' can be a collection of rotting wood, corroded aluminium, tatty fabric, bent sheet aluminium *et al*, that is awaiting rebuilding by an enthusiast group. Sometimes you will hear in even more hushed terms, a 'Classic Veteran Aircraft'. This is one from any period from 1903 to 1980 that has been recovered from any of the places previously mentioned, or even a great hole in the ground, and rebuilt so that it actually flies again. Most of these will be found either in the hands of eccentric millionaires or The Shuttleworth Collection, which are actually two VERY different things.

'These fine TVs going to the large gentleman for £5000. Sold. What am I bid for this decrepit old aeroplane?' PRM

'Just because it's sponsored by British Coal, there's no need to go to these lengths you know.' PRM

Victor

When Victor K2 XM715 was retired to Bruntingthorpe it used the radio call sign 'Meldrew 1'. Was this because it had 'one foot in the grave'? It now has the appropriate nose art. NIGEL SCOINES

Video Cameras and Camcorders

Now fast assuming pre-eminence as a medium for visually recording aircraft and air events, the video camera/camcorder is actually a bit of a mixed blessing, insofar as while the idea may be a good one, the execution of it isn't. In fact, not to put too fine a point on it, that Jeremy Beadle bloke's got a lot to answer for. It's bad enough that he encourages people to go out and make complete fools of themselves so that the rest of us can laugh at their misfortunes. What is worse is that he seems hell-bent on encouraging anybody who happens to have more money than sense to buy one of the damned things.

It's getting to the stage where you can't even go to the toilet without some wally with a camcorder turning up and filming you. You might think this an exaggeration, but at the local supermarket the other day there was some clown busily filming his wife while she did the week's shopping. What made it even more infuriating was that she was filming him filming her, while there was also a BBC crew doing a film report on the growth of camcorders filming them filming each other. About the only thing missing was Esther Rantzen and her obsession with funny-shaped vegetables.

If Anneka Rice wants a REAL challenge, why doesn't she do something really useful and arrange for all known camcorders to be returned to their maker. This would be of great benefit to most aviation enthusiasts, who consider anyone with a camcorder at an airshow an absolute menace. You have only to watch them at any air event to get a clear understanding of how far the camcorder has taken over their lives. Here's a short list of the types most commonly found at events of this kind.

The Imaginary BBC Producer: He (or she) seems to have absolutely no regard for anybody else whatsoever. Indeed, they seem to take positive delight in getting in the way of anyone using a still camera. This is usually accomplished by hiding behind something and then jumping out to begin filming at the exact nano-second at which the photographer depresses the shutter release button. They are utterly impervious to abusive remarks. Worse still, since they can re-use video tape, it is quite impossible to get one's own back by pulling this stunt in reverse and jumping out in front of them. About the only effective countermeasure is fixing magnets to their camcorder with superglue.

Russian Air Force formation video team in action. LINDSAY PEACOCK

The Imaginary BBC Producer (Mk.II): Similar to the above, but takes twice as long and always gets in the way of the ordinary photographer whenever the sun comes out. Appears to be profoundly deaf whenever the sun is shining, since earnest entreaties to move are ignored until the exact moment that the sun disappears again. At that moment, he (or she) will suddenly realise that 47 photographers are screaming abuse at them. He (or she) will then smile sweetly and walk off without an apology. The above scenario will then be re-enacted at every possible opportunity.

The Imaginary BBC Producer (Mk.III): Like the above, but with a more professional rig that includes a boom microphone. In case you are not familiar with boom microphones, they are those things that look like a pole, upon which some sort of fluffy animal has been painfully impaled. The boom microphone will invariably be carried by an assistant, who will wave it about enthusiastically and make sure it appears in pictures taken by at least 25 still photographers. Boom microphone assistants are also adept at using them for defensive purposes – and if you have ever been struck on the head by a boom microphone, you will be aware that it can be a painful experience, since they are only fluffy on the outside.

The Novice: This, without doubt, is the most dangerous one of the lot, being a menace to himself (or herself) and everyone else. Spends most of the time walking around with the camera held in place adjacent to the eye, an act which greatly impairs the field of vision. In consequence, the Novice usually has no idea where he (or she) is going. In normal situations this might not be a problem. At an airshow, it's a nightmare for the Novice repeatedly bumps into anything that gets in the way – members of the crowd, fences and barricades, photographers, rubbish bins, portaloos, aircraft and helicopters, other camcorder operators, BBC film crews, cars, sales stands, you name it, they'll bump into it. In the process of ricocheting off everything not in sight, they soon learn to ignore the rules of courtesy – which is why you will never receive an apology for anything from anyone who is carrying a camcorder, so there's no point in standing there open-mouthed after being steam-rollered out of the way by one of these people. Chances are, they didn't even see you.

Force

This was the British Government's answer to the present day American 'A Team' as seen on frequent ITV repeats. It was a group of bombers flown by intrepid birdmen, ready to fly at the slightest whim of the Prime Minister, to any troubled spot in the world and wash the British dirty linen in public. Hence it became known as the 'British Detergent'. This role was eventually handed over to the Royal Navy, as they were more at home in hot water and in any case parts of the 'V' Bombers began to corrode – due no doubt to the use of the wrong washing powder, or the introduction of fabric softeners. Also many preservation groups had their eyes on them thus giving the Chancellor the opportunity to make a quick pound or two for the Government's coffers.

Now that the Government has officially said that Tornados will no longer carry even the tiniest of nuclear bombs, we can

'This damned thing is sapping my strength.' PRM

tell you that the RAF's WE177 bomb is in fact (as its service name suggests) a Wee Replica, one seventy-seventh scale, of the first British atomic weapon dropped from a Vickers Valiant on the poor unfortunates in the Australian Desert near Woomera.

Pilot to navigator 'Are you SURE that is Port Stanley down there?' PRM

Warbirds

'Great Scott, we haven't room for that lot on the Champagne Flight.'
ANDREW MARCH

'I said light her up – not burn her up.' PRM

'Daddy, why is Mr Farewell sponsoring the Vulcan?' PRM

'Go get in your Spitfire, we could do a replay.' BRIAN STRICKLAND

'These cut price home-built jet warbirds will never catch on.' PRM

'Thank you General for this generous gesture – this fighter will fill the gap very well until we get the Eurofighter 2022.' PRM

'They didn't half make these WW2 planes difficult to get into.'
BRIAN STRICKLAND

Weather

Modern forecasters are able to avail themselves of all sorts of high technology equipment including computers and radar as tools to assist in the vital business of predicting the weather, but I sometimes wonder if they simply forget to look out the window. I make this point on the basis that the weather I get seldom seems to bear any relationship (living or dead) to the weather predicted for me by Michael Fish, Bill Giles, Kenneth McKellar, Suzanne Vega, Rob McElwheeeeee and others of that ilk.

Mind you, having said that, you have to admit that they do lie so convincingly and, in one or two cases, so charmingly as well. If I wasn't such a cynic, I'd be inclined to think that they actually believe what they're saying – but that would surely be stretching credibility too far, wouldn't it?

'We always recommend you bring your sun shade to Fairford.'
BRIAN STRICKLAND

'Portable weather stations are all the rage. You can decide looking at your windsock which end of the runway to go to.' BRIAN ATKINSON

Weather Herk

When the RAF first received its 66 C-130K Hercules some 30 years ago, one of the aircraft was found to have a recurring problem – its nose drooped. When this occurred in flight the Herk became almost uncontrollable. The ever resourceful engineers at the RAE decided that a longer, pointed nose would alleviate the problem. However, to fit the contours of the C-130's proboscis the pointed nose turned out to be very long. It had to be painted with candy stripes to prevent aircrew and vehicles from colliding with it. Of course the nose radar didn't work now so it was moved above the cockpit. *Snoopy*, as it was called by the affectionate engineers who had spent many hours working on it, was now ready to join the rest of the fleet.

Of course it looked so unusual and different from all the other Herks, that it was immediately ostracised by them. It became more and more unhappy at Lyneham, where the engineers couldn't puzzle out why there were always pools of water underneath it, day and night. Eventually the powers that be called an emergency meeting to decide what should happen to this C-130. "Whether we find some other use for it, or chop it up to

Well prepared, the C-130 Weather Herk carries a spare nose job wherever it goes. GRAHAM FINCH

make a simulator must be decided very quickly," said the station commander to his senior staff. "Bingo, you've got it right there sir," responded young Flight Lieutenant Stephen Screen, "Weather". "Whether what?" retorted Wg Cdr Barrie Meter, his blood pressure rising somewhat. "Replace that clapped out old Hastings for our trips to Macrihanish for kippers, ski trips to Norway and the

The crew can be instantly recognised (night or day) by their headgear, that has been screwed into place and is only removed to have their hair cut. JEREMY FLACK

occasional trans-Atlantic jaunt, sir. You could get your car in the back of Snoopy, it will save hiring one at the other end." And so it came to pass – the very special C–130 went back to Farnborough and replaced the Hastings, ostensibly for weather research. You can still see it today, operating the new Distant Ranging Aircraft (DRA) charter and executive flights from Boscombe Down. Whether this continues much longer is anyone's guess. No doubt the government will decided to privatise it and bring about a change in the weather (Herk). The flightcrew, and their distinctive uniforms, will be sorry to see this very (personally) profitable enterprise blown away and subsumed into yet another British Airways Express operation. Come on all you environmentally conscious enthusiasts, write a letter to your MP extolling the virtues of the weather Hercules. It's doing a great job for us out there somewhere, and we want to see it at IAT year after year.

Westland

Westland-SIKORSKY S-55 Fishing helicopter. An instant success until the Spanish started cutting its lines and throwing their oars into the rotor blades. PRM

Yes Westland did design the Westminster, shown at Farnborough in 1958 – but they were unable to get it finished in time and the passengers all fell out. PRM

Westland-SIKORSKY S-55 Car transporter. A product of the popular urge to cross the Channel before the Chunnel was dug out, but it was just too slow with one car at a time. PRM

Now Britain's only helicopter manufacturer, Westland Helicopters at Yeovil is the world's most successful company at building other people's designs. Its passage through the 50 years of helicopter production in the UK has seen it assemble large numbers of Sikorsky S-51s, S-55s, S-58s and S-61s (or Dragonflies, Whirlwinds, Wessex and Sea Kings if you like); it subsumed Bristol Helicopters – and built Sycamores and Belvederes; Fairey and Saunders Roe and built Scouts and Wasps and more recently has collaborated with Sud Aviation/Aerospatiale to build Gazelles and Pumas. Even the

Westland-SIKORSKY S-58 seen here performing the dramatic rescue of somebody's mother-in-law. PRM

Wheels

The wheel is one of the most essential parts of an aeroplane (not a helicopter – that can make do with a couple of planks of wood; nor a flying boat that has a hull). Aircraft wheels were invented by the rubber companies, to ease unemployment. They designed rubber rings and soon discovered that some wood or metal was needed in the middle to stop them collapsing when the pilot tried to land his plane. They called this an aero-wheel. The first square ones were not successful, nor were the oval ones that followed (you must have seen early film of aircraft trying to land with oval wheels and bouncing to destruction).

They even tried copying the Russian Mi-24 Hind! It just didn't get off the ground. PRM

Lynx, the nearest thing to a wholly designed and built helicopter was part of an Anglo-French agreement. We won't mention the Westland Westminster or the more recent WG30 (otherwise known as *The Vibrator*) and Lynx 3. You can find a true testimony to these machines at the excellent International Helicopter Museum at Weston-super-Mare. And for the future – the troubled EH101 Merlin (two of the nine prototypes already lost before it enters service) is a joint adventure with Agusta in Italy. To date, only the British Government has had the courage to order it for the RN and a very reluctant RAF. Westland's factory at Yeovil is likely to see out the decade producing McDonnell Douglas Apaches or some other Army attack helicopter.

The original square wheel supports around the outside were not successful. The expression 'dog-tyred' has, however, remained.

Early flight trials to reduce rotor vibration were unsuccessful. Removal of the final blade, however, drastically affected lift. PRM

The successful outcome came from a Mr Dun Lop, a Chinese test pilot seconded to de Havilland at Stag Lane in the 1930s. He was fed up with hard landings in the DH Moth, particularly as he suffered from an uncomfortable infliction on account of the English food. So he took his daughter We Lee's inflatable rubber rings that she used for swimming lessons and fitted them round a Moth's wheels. He found them a great improvement and wrote a note to his boss afterwards – 'Dun Lop retires from hard landings, We Lees round soft rubbers very successful cushions.'

'The single-mainwheel performance of the Spitfire was so erratic that its use on the later U-2 (qv) is remarkable. PAUL JARRETT

The solid wheels were not to Dun Lop's liking (above) but fitting his daughter's inflatable swimming rings round the wheels made him much more comfortable when landing the Moth (below). These photos are printed large because the compiler is a lepidopterist! PRM

Wing Walking

Clearly, referring to these immobilised individuals as being engaged in the act of wing-walking is yet another one of those irritating contradictions in terms that appear to abound in the aeronautical world. They should really be known as "wing-standing" acts or as 'wing-strapped-firmly-in-place-but-still-able-to-wave-gaily-at-the-plebs' acts. Such a description might not have the same exciting buzz, but it would be more than compensated for by the virtue of accuracy.

Wing-walkers – RAF style. PRM

The latest USAF wing-walking team prepares for its debut, briefed by the Captain. PRM

For added power on take-off, this 'wing-walker' converts into an extra propeller. PRM

Women Pilots

'There I was – the Hun was on my tail....' BRIAN STRICKLAND

After glamour decorating the outside of the cockpit ....

we now have glamour in the cockpit as well.

Another potential minefield so we had better be careful with any funny remarks. Women are generally better drivers than men, although you'll seldom get a man to agree with that sentiment – unless he happens to be an insurance salesman and we all know what awful wimps they are. Women are also much safer drivers than men, so there appears to be no obvious reason

why they shouldn't make better pilots too. For the benefit of keeping the compiler out of trouble we will state quite emphatically that 'women pilots have a delicate touch, high intelligence level, superb physical shape and understanding of all things mechanical' making them the best pilots in the world. Getting them to exceed 50mph, however, might be a problem.

I wonder what Flt Lt Jo Salter will choose to paint on the outside of her No 617 Squadron 'Dambusters' Tornado? PRM

X-Planations

Some more of those vital questions that the REAL aviation enthusiast needs to be able to answer.

● Who invented the airship?

No, not Herr Hindenburg, Count von Zeppelin nor Led Zeppelin. It was Leonardo da Vinci – who actually invented everything to do with flying.

Leonardo can be thanked for the airship – and many more flying objects. PRM

● What is the most spectacular solo aerobatic performance given by a multi-engined aircraft?

There have been several fantastic barrel rolls by DC-8s and Boeing 707s, usually for films. Roly Falk gave a stunning performance in the Vulcan at Farnborough. But the international credit goes to Bob Hoover who has for many years given a full aerobatic display in a Shrike Commander, including loops and rolls with both engines stopped and landing and taxying in to his parking spot *before* starting them up again.

This is one Hoover that makes a silent pass without ending up in a pile of dirt. PRM

● How does an airliner's captain control the aircraft when his co-pilot is having lunch and he wishes to relieve himself?

He attaches string to the control column and tweaks the ends of the string (as you would a kite's strings) if he feels the aircraft is diverting from its course.

● How does a pilot of an airliner navigate when it's dark and his electronic systems fail?

He follows the street lights now that most motorways have them. If it's cloudy he tunes his pocket radio into the BBC and homes in on it. Should he be really stuck he takes out his brand new GPS (Global Positioning System) from its box, reads the instructions and if he presses all the right buttons, it tells him his exact position. He then uses his pocket mobile phone to telephone the nearest airfield and shouts help.

X-Planes

It was customary in 1945 to name all experimental aircraft X–planes, particularly in the USA where there were aircraft like the X-5, X-15 and so on. In England they tended to think that aviation had reached the limit of human endurance and the Government of the day banned all experimental manned aircraft

Flying aircraft like this is eXhilirating for the crews, eXciting for the spectators, and a fine eXample of eXhibitionism at its best. Get too close though, and it all gets awfully eXpensive.

that were planned to investigate supersonic flight. So X-planes took on a new meaning in the UK where the term referred to a pile of scrap or a hole in the ground. This is probably when the very first seeds of the preservation movement were sown. It also led to a new approach by those who just will not accept that biplane is dead; the result is that in the film Star Wars the 'X–wing' fighter made its debut.

If you study this fighter carefully you will see that it is in fact a biplane with its four sets of wings arranged in a different configuration. Watch out for the Jedi otherwise before long a secret group will be started to prove that the Tiger Moth with an RB211 engine would be a suitable MRCA for replacing the Tornado. Those of you with satellite or cable TV will also well know that the X-Planes series on the Discovery Channel (repeated on every alternate day ending in Y for the past five years and probably for the next five as well), is an excellent series portraying the story of the X-1 to the X-15, with a bit more thrown in for good measure.

-Rays

These are a source of constant concern to REAL aviation photographers as they travel the world in search of fascinating subjects to point their lenses at. Why? Because of the sensitivity of their photographic film in their camera bags to bombardment by x-rays at airports. Most machines used for examining hand luggage state that they do no harm to film – but what they don't say is that they can have a cumulative effect. A journey across Europe from West to East with plenty of photo stopovers can damage your film – particularly the ex-Soviet Union made machines (using the by-products from Chernobyl). Many photographers have learned how to out-wit the machine minders using 'special techniques'. This is all the more worrying as this same method could be used to conceal more sinister objects in hand luggage. That's why we aren't going into more detail here.

Yaks

Yaks grazing at North Weald. PRM

These untidy looking beasts have escaped from the Russian Steppes in appreciable numbers over the last few years. They used to migrate as far as the Berlin Wall, but failed to get past it, thus protecting Western Europe from their competition for the meagre amounts of airfield grass. However, once the wall came down there has been nothing to stop them and they've even crossed the English Channel to invade our shores. Reports from around the country of Yak-watchers show some disturbing figures. Duxford Yaks – 11, North Weald & Wellesbourne Mountford Yaks – 52, Compton Abbas & Little Gransden Yaks – 18, White Waltham Yaks – 55. It is even reported that a Mark Jefferies is breeding them on his farm in Bedfordshire. Beware, no grass airfield will soon be without its Yak, elbowing the indiginous Beagle or the few surviving Camels and Gazelles out of the way. Let's hope that the CAA appreciates the enormity of the problem and brings in its Hunters with their Hawks and Falcons or even ask the FAA to send in an Eagle or two, to chase the Yaks away.

Youth

Most airshow organisers have learned how to deal with ATC cadets who pose as REAL enthusiasts. BRIAN STRIKCLAND

As with nearly all things, there is always a twist in the tail. By now you have nearly become a REAL enthusiast, but be very wary, you are not quite there. Be very, very careful about the biggest danger to all aspiring aviation buffs: Members of the Air Training Corps, or ATC for short. These pimply faced masters, and now misses, cannot be taken on face value, they will quote you wing-loading factors, static thrust, every aspect of aerodynamics, the ins-and-outs of RADAR, heat-seeking missiles, the histories of every aircraft built, and some not built, in fact everything to do with aviation. They will almost certainly also be crack marksmen, and faster over 220 yards than you are over 25 yards. Forget their angelic looks, and avoid any reference to your interest in aviation within their earshot. It is much better to claim a deep and avid interest in the letters of the younger Pliny; even then you might occasionally be on dangerous ground.

Air Scouts can be equally dangerous and will also know a lot about knots and starting fires by rubbing two aviation enthusiasts together.

A mating pair of Yaks about to go off in search of new pastures. ANDREW MARCH

Z-Cars

'Suppose it's a good idea to have a Pitts to fly inverted to see what's going on below.' PRM

Readers old enough to remember this long-running TV police series will not be surprised at the use of this heading. The police have gone a long way since the introduction of pandas to replace their bicycles. Sadly the reproduction of pandas has virtually ceased since they saw themselves on TV in black and white. With the Chinese now having a complete monopoly and tension rising in Hong Kong with 1997 approaching, police forces have had to resort to shanks' pony or squirrels for their mobility. Some of the larger police forces have been able to purchase these Aerospatiale Squirrels and others have introduced MBB Bo105 Beetles.

The poorer Police Authorities have had to make do and mend as they can. One of the most unusual eye in the sky 'Crimestoppers' is a Pitts Special built at home by PC I S Pottem in his garden at Chipping Sodbury. He had the idea when he saw Brian Lecomber flying his Pitts upside-down, waving to the crowd at an airshow. "It's ideal," he said, "the Pitts flies just as well upside-down as the right way up. When you want to stop a stolen car you just invert the Pitts and fly low over the car and wave the driver to pull in and stop." Police forces around the country are studying the initial trials of this new Z-car, currently in service with the Scilly Isles Force.

ZZZZZzzzzzzzzzz... ... ...

Symbol used by navigators to show they were asleep during the briefing ... If you have got this far, you should now have a basic grounding on which to build your career as a REAL aviation enthusiast. If you require more ... hey you ... are you awake?

'Hang on a jiff. Must get to the end of the chapter.' R FORSEY

Asleep? – No he's just pretending – I think. He didn't react though when the Concorde took off, so maybe he's brain dead instead.
RICHARD COOPER

A REAL aviation journalist at work, he's enjoying the show dreaming about... well that's another story. DANIEL MARCH

Oh well, I guess there is always gardening or shopping to occupy summer Saturdays and Sundays ... No, don't wake up, I'll see myself out ... Enjoy yourself!